But What If I Don't Want to Go to College?

A Guide to Success Through Alternative Education

Harlow G. Unger

Facts On File®

AN INFOBASE HOLDINGS COMPANY

But What If I Don't Want to Go to College?

Facts On File, Inc.
460 Park Avenue South
New York, NY 10016

Library of Congress Cataloging-in-Publication Data
Unger, Harlow G., 1931–
   But what if I don't want to go to college? : a guide to success through alternative education / Harlow G. Unger.
      p.   cm
   Includes index.
   ISBN 0-8160-2534-7 (hc)
   ISBN 0-8160-2836-2 (pbk)
   1. Occupational training—United States. 2. Vocational education—United States. 3. Non-formal education—United States. 4. Vocational guidance—United States. I. Title.
HD5715.2.U53 1991
370.11'3'0973—dc20   91-3186

Facts On File books are available at special discounts when purchased in bulk quantities for businesses, associations, institutions or sales promotions. Please call our Special Sales Department in New York at 212/683-2244 or 800/322-8755.

Text design by Ron Monteleone
Cover design by Catherine Hyman
Jacket design by Carla Weise/Levavi & Levavi, Inc.

Printed in the United States of America

MP VC 10 9 8 7 6 5

This book is printed on acid-free paper.

But What If I Don't Want to
Go to College?

About the Author

Harlow G. Unger has written two other books on education, *"What Did You Learn in School Today?"* and *A Student's Guide to College Admissions—Everything Your Guidance Counselor Has No Time to Tell You*, both published by Facts On File. A graduate of Yale University and former adjunct professor at two New York–area colleges, Unger spent more than 30 years as a journalist and foreign correspondent—a craft that required no college degree when he began.

To my friends
of many seasons and many years

Dobie and Lorry
Gene, Chuck and Ted
Lorraine and Cherie
Ron and Kathy
Liz

and

Henrietta and Al Hendrick
who inspired this book

Contents

Acknowledgments

The author wishes to express his thanks to those whose help made this book possible: Mrs. Henrietta Hendrick, Career Information Office, Rockland County Guidance Center, Nyack, NY; Mr. Mark Schwartz and Dr. Tom White, U.S. Department of Education, Washington, DC; Dr. Mary Cross, National Center for Research in Vocational Education, Washington, DC; Mr. Patrick F. Todd, National Commission for Cooperative Education; Mr. Joseph S. Carris, Executive Search Consultant, New York; Ms. Kathy Ishizuka, Project Editor, Facts On File, New York, NY; and Ms. Paula Diamond, The Paula Diamond Agency, New York, NY.

Upon the education of the people of this country the fate of this country depends.

— Benjamin Disraeli

PART I

---

*Career Education—Alternative
Routes to Success*

Chapter 1

College Isn't for Everyone

Nurses, computer operators, chefs, plumbers, air traffic controllers, actors, mechanics, barbers, glaziers, security guards, bank tellers, firefighters, clerks, telephone operators, carpenters, postal workers, railroad engineers, masons, police officers, telephone and electric company linepeople, meat cutters, travel agents, dental technicians . . .

How could our towns, cities and nation—how could our world—get along without the talents and skills of the brilliant men and women who fill these and hundreds of other jobs? The answer is we couldn't, and all who are thinking of joining these important professions should be proud of the vital contributions they'll make to our world.

Aside from their essential nature, all of these jobs have something else in common: None requires a four-year college or university degree. Some don't even require any schooling after high school—even at a two-year community college. That doesn't mean any of these jobs is easy. No important job ever is. All require hard work, dedication, knowledge, intelligence and on-the-job training. But, as in most occupations, success not only yields a sense of professional pride and accomplishment, it can yield considerable financial rewards—again, without ever going to college.

Anyone who wants to can go to college, but not every one wants to, and not everyone should go—certainly not for four years. There are about 1,200 two-year and 2,200 four-year colleges in the United States, and the vast majority admits almost everybody who applies. So, it's easy to get into college. But 50% of students at four-year colleges and universities quit without ever graduating, and more than half of all college seniors fail tests that measure basic knowledge of history, literature and foreign languages. So not everyone who goes to college belongs there.

The fact is millions of students all over the world are not suited for and have no interest in traditional academic schooling—which is why alternative career education was developed: to teach students the

3

skills they need to get a good job. German and Japanese schools automatically test all 14-year-olds to determine their aptitudes. Such tests let the academically skilled continue traditional schooling, while students with other talents move into alternative forms of education— career education that refines those talents and insures their becoming successful, respected artisans and craftspeople.

Many U.S. schools offer the same choice, but a lot of students automatically reject alternative education because well-meaning, but often misguided, friends, teachers, counselors and parents pressure them to stick to traditional academics and go to four-year colleges to get a "good" job. The truth is that a four-year college is only one route to a good job. There are many other routes that can lead to the same or even greater success and personal fulfillment than jobs requiring college degrees. Indeed, of the 20 fastest growing occupations, according to the U.S. Department of Labor, few require a four-year university degree. Most, as you can see in Table 1, are occupations for which the required training is available in career education programs in good high schools, two-year community and junior colleges and in technical institutes. By the year 2000, there will be 3 million more jobs in the hospitality industry, one million more jobs in the construction trade and 850,000 more jobs for nurse's aides and other health technicians. The market for computer service and repair technicians will grow from 500,000 to 750,000 in the next five years alone. Jobs for college professors, on the other hand, will shrink by 4%.

Right now, as you read this book, our country is facing acute shortages of skilled production workers, electronic and electrical technicians, tool and die makers, machine tool maintenance and repair workers, medical technicians and technicians in other fields. Those shortages are a key reason some U.S. industries are finding it difficult to effectively compete with companies in Japan, Germany and other countries, where career education is better developed and respected than in the United States. But that's beginning to change, and many American companies now offer graduates of the best technical and vocational education programs as much as they offer university graduates.

Despite all the publicity about "high-tech," pure high-technology jobs account for only about 5% to 6% of all jobs in the United States; and executive, administrative and managerial positions requiring uni-

WHERE THE NEW JOBS WILL BE

Table 1. The U.S. Department of Labor estimates that the 20 fastest growing occupations in the United States listed below will create more than 14 million new jobs between now and the year 2000. Most will be for graduates of vocational education programs.

Industry	New Jobs
Eating and drinking places	2,471,000
Offices of health practitioners	1,375,000
New construction, repairs and renovations	890,000
Nursing and personal care facilities	852,000
Personnel supply services	832,000
State and local government education	784,000
Machinery and equipment wholesalers	614,000
Computer and data processing services	613,000
Grocery stores	596,000
Hotels and other lodging places	574,000
Outpatient facilities and health services	547,000
State and local general government	546,000
Research, management and consulting services	531,000
Legal services	522,000
Credit agencies and investment offices	499,000
Credit reporting and business services	497,000
Hospitals, private	481,000
Department stores	386,000
Real estate	353,000
Services to dwellings and other buildings	341,000

Source: U.S. Department of Labor, Bureau of Labor Statistics

versity degrees account for only 23% of all jobs. Technical, sales and administrative support jobs account for 31% of all jobs, while precision production, craft and repair personnel fill about 13%. More than one-third of all jobs are filled by machine operators, fabricators, assemblers, inspectors, transportation workers, handlers, equipment cleaners, laborers, protective service workers, civil service workers (including firefighters and police officers), household and hospitality workers, agricultural workers (farming, forestry and fishing) and workers in other service occupations. In other words, more than 70% of all jobs in the United States only require alternative career education and on-the-job training.

The fact is there are only two good reasons for going to a four-year college or university: a deep desire to study traditional academic subjects (literature, history, philosophy, languages, science, and so on) or a deep commitment to career goals that can only be reached with a university education (law, medicine and similar professions).

So if you're one of the millions of Americans who really don't want to or need to go to a university, and your talents and career goals are in areas not requiring a university degree, by all means consider alternative career education. Alternative education can open thousands of career opportunities in the arts, crafts, science and health care, sports, skilled trades, manufacturing, construction, travel, banking and finance and even in your own business—and there's no need to spend thousands of dollars and four precious years at a university if you don't really need to or want to.

What Is Alternative Education?

In simplest terms, alternative education is practical training that will convert your basic skills, talents and interests into a good job and a lasting, rewarding career. Alternative education will help you become a master craftsperson—an expert everyone wants and needs to hire.

Like traditional academics, alternative education is available through courses at almost every level of schooling—high school, community college, technical institutes and four-year colleges and universities. But it's also available in apprenticeship programs and on-the-job training programs provided by many companies and labor unions. In many cases, alternative education involves no formal classroom study . There are many career opportunities where alternative education simply involves getting an entry-level job in which you earn while you learn—and the more you learn, the more you earn. More than one-quarter of all factory workers and one-third of all tradeworkers, craftspeople and office and clerical workers learn their skills on the job.

How much alternative education you'll need in an area will largely depend on the demands of your work and your employer—and your own interests. In some areas, you may want to continue learning new skills and improving old ones all your life. Some industries require skills that can be learned entirely in high school. Others require skills taught only at technical schools or community colleges, because high schools either don't teach them or don't teach advanced levels. Still other courses are available at four-year colleges and universities, where alternative education students may take them on a full-time or part-time basis during the day or evening, with or without studying for a degree.

And that's what this book is about: to show you exactly what type of alternative career education is available, where to get it and how much you'll need to get your first job in a wide variety of careers. The rest of this section will tell you all about alternative education—how to evaluate it and how to pick the right career track for you. Remember: Career education is worthless if it can't help you get a job. Part II lists hundreds of career and talent areas that do not require four-year college or university degrees for entry-level jobs and a clear track to success. Each career listing includes the education or training needed to get started, the pay range and some companies and organizations that need those skills. Part III will show you how to get started in your new career area, with some easy-to-use tips for applying for, and getting, your first job: writing a good resume, completing a successful job application and using the job interview to sell yourself and your talents.

One important thing to keep in mind as you read ahead is that there are almost no limits to the personal *and* financial rewards available from the opportunities described in this book. Even jobs that only pay minimum wage to start can lead to opportunities in management and ownership after you've learned enough about your new craft or trade. Almost all owners and managers started out as ordinary workers in their trades and businesses. Many restaurant owners were once waiters, many store owners started as stock clerks and salespeople and many successful building contractors started as laborers or apprentices. The same is true for managers and owners in almost all of the trades and businesses in Part II, and they got to the top without spending four years at college. You can too. Let's find out how—and good luck!

Getting Started

One exciting thing about alternative education is that it is basically open to all. There are no age limits, for example, and almost no background requirements. To sign up—and to succeed—all you really need is an interest in and a desire to learn a craft or trade. You can start at 16 or 60, whenever *you* are ready. Adults of any age, regardless of educational background, may enroll in virtually every type of program, whether it's on the job, at a two- or four-year college or at a local public high school or technical school. Indeed, more than one-third of all community college students and public vocational high school students are more than 30 years old. Most programs are available on weekends and at night as well as during the day, so as not to interfere with any job you may have. More than 60% of community college students are enrolled part-time.

Alternative education programs are also available to college students who want to switch from traditional academics or who wish to combine traditional academics with alternative education. High school students often have the same choices: They can switch from traditional academic programs to vocational education or combine the two. So, no matter how old you are or what your circumstances—whether you're in school or not—alternative education programs are open to you. It's only a question of finding the right one.

Even if you've already left high school without getting a diploma, or left so long ago you can't remember what you learned there, you can still take advantage of alternative education. Many alternative education programs don't require a high school diploma for admission. What you may want to consider, however, is enrolling in an equivalency diploma program to brush up on and master basic reading, writing and calculating skills while you take alternative education. Combining the two will give you a marketable skill *and* a high school diploma—a combination guaranteed to open the door to endless opportunities that await all bright, talented, hard-working men and women. Chapter 2 shows you how to get your equivalency diploma, and how to evaluate *yourself,* especially if you're convinced you have no skills. Everyone has skills and talents, and you do too! The problem is that not everyone knows how to determine what his or her talents are. One way is to identify your interests first. Whatever they are—sports, rock music or science—there are endless jobs to match those interests, even if you're not an athlete, musician or scientist. There are hundreds of vital jobs in every field, and, with alternative education, it's easy to learn how to do them. So keep reading!

Combining Career Education and College

Although none of the career opportunities in this book require a four-year college degree, if you want to go to college or to a university, by all means do so. College can provide you with a useful and rewarding education, and it may, if you're not sure yet, help you determine how you want to spend the rest of your life. Most colleges are like enormous cafeterias of knowledge, offering endless choices of courses in traditional academics as well as preprofessional and alternative education. Many people, for one reason or another, often fail to recognize the value of traditional academics—the liberal arts. Often it's because they may have had some poor or boring teachers in high school, and they assume they won't enjoy or get anything out of further study in the liberal arts. But the liberal arts are designed to help students develop intellectual and creative abilities that will prove valuable in almost every occupation.

So, you can combine the best of many educational worlds at college and "taste" different areas of knowledge before you make any career decisions. What's more, about 1,000 two- and four-year colleges across the United States now participate with local industries in the growing cooperative education movement to provide a mixture of liberal arts and practical arts education that will assure graduates of immediate jobs at cooperating companies. The exciting career opportunities available through cooperative education are described in the second half of this chapter.

Remember, too, that no matter what career you eventually choose, a degree from a two-year or four-year college will always be a big plus on your resume.

But don't enroll in a full-time, four-year or even two-year college simply because others want or expect you to. For many, college can be the happiest years and worth every penny of tuition invested in it. For others, college can mean years of misery and a waste of a family's life savings. Remember, 50% of U.S. college students drop out without ever getting a degree.

Only you can decide whether you will benefit more from college, alternative education or a combination of both. I hope this book will help you make that decision. One decision to avoid at all costs, however, is to pursue *no* education, either academic or vocational—in other words, to quit school. Fifty years ago, a decision to quit school and go to work at age 16 or 18 was perfectly sound for many people, because there were many jobs for unskilled workers. Elevators in almost every department store and office and apartment building had to be operated by hand. Streets were swept, roads were built and crops were harvested—all by hand. In offices and stores everywhere, all books were kept by hand. Most of this is no longer true. Elevators run automatically; machines sweep streets, pave roads and harvest crops. And most sales at a supermarket or department store checkout are punched into a cash register, which automatically feeds all data into a computer that maintains the bookkeeping and provides calculated printouts at the touch of a button.

There are almost no more job opportunities for unskilled workers, because there are almost no more unskilled jobs. Indeed, unemployment rates among the unskilled—those who dropped out of high school without getting their diplomas—is 25%, compared to a 15% unemployment rate for high school graduates, a 9% unemployment rate for people with one to three years of college and 6% for people with degrees from four-year colleges. No one can afford to consider quitting school anymore. The only decisions for intelligent people today is what kind of school to attend, what kind of education to get—academic, vocational or a combination of both—and how much education to get.

Keep in mind that the decision you make is not irreversible. It will naturally be less costly in time and money if you can decide what you'll do the rest of your life before you graduate from high school. But most people don't, and that's a fact. To prove it, just ask your parents or teachers whether they are now doing exactly what they planned to do when they were 16 or 17 years old. The chances are they're not, and, if you're still in high school, it's unfair to expect you to know what you're going to do 25 years from now.

For most people, the decision that seems right at one particular time is often not right at another time. So, if you make a decision now and find you're unhappy about it later on, there is absolutely no reason to feel badly about changing your mind and starting on a new course. It's important to remain flexible and be prepared to change with time and circumstances.

If you decide that vocational education is right for you at this time in your life and others disapprove of your decision, show them this book so they can see how alternative education can help you develop skills and talents to take advantage of rewarding career opportunities. There are many careers that don't require a college education but do provide millions all over the world with successful, rewarding lives. You must fulfill *your* ambitions, not those of your parents or friends or anyone else.

What Kind of Alternative Education Is Best?

Before exploring specific career opportunities, let's look at the various types of alternative education open to you and see how to evaluate them. Careful evaluation is the key to getting good alternative education. Just because your local high school or community college offers vocational courses does not mean you'll gain any useful knowledge if you take them. According to U.S. government studies, more than half the students who take high school vocational courses graduate with obsolete, *useless* skills (see Table 2). So just because a high school or college counselor says a vocational course or program is good doesn't make it good. And just because a vocational school advertises on television doesn't make it good or even honest. Many private trade schools that advertise on television are operated by con artists—which is why careful evaluation of alternative education programs is so important. Many students have wasted their time and life savings pursuing useless vocational education programs. Many have gone into debt without learning useful job skills. Let's make sure that doesn't happen to you.

Let's look at the various kinds of alternative education available, and then at ways to find out if they're any good. There are 10 basic sources of vocational education. Although many are not available in most communities, it's important that you know them by name so you can recognize them. They are:

1. Comprehensive high schools
2. Specialized vocational/technical (vo-tech) high schools

3. Cooperative education programs
    a. High schools
    b. Colleges
4. "Two-plus-two" tech-prep programs
5. Community colleges
6. Technical institutes
7. Private, not-for-profit junior (two-year) colleges
8. Private, for-profit (proprietary) trade schools
9. Four-year colleges and universities
10. Employer/union apprenticeship programs
11. Employer-sponsored training programs

Let's take a closer look at each of them and at their advantages and disadvantages. Then let's try to work out the best possible program for you.

1. Comprehensive high schools. A comprehensive high school is an ordinary high school—the kind students attend everywhere in the United States. Almost all offer vocational courses as well as academic courses, and about 30% of all high school students are in vocational education programs. Many programs offer evening as well as daytime courses and welcome adults. As stated before, more than one-third of the students in high school vocational education programs are more than 30 years old.

ADVANTAGES: These programs offer an early opportunity to learn about a trade or occupation without making a long-term commitment. High school vocational education allows for an easy transition from academics without having to switch to a new school and make new friends.

DISADVANTAGES: Unless tied to a high school cooperative education program (see Number 3), the vast majority of vocational education programs in comprehensive high schools are, by themselves, inadequate. Almost half the vocational training offered by comprehensive high schools is in agriculture, home economics and industrial arts—areas in which the number of jobs is shrinking. Few train students for jobs as technicians, who are most in demand in virtually every industry. Moreover, most comprehensive high schools usually teach only one or two courses in each occupational area, and that's simply not enough education to get a good job. Many high school vocational courses and teachers lack up-to-date training, resources, equipment and methods. Although more than one-quarter of all high school students are enrolled in vocational education courses in comprehensive high schools, most emerge from these courses with obsolete job skills, and many employers do not honor high school diplomas received for vocational education. As one U.S. government report put it, the typical high school vocational education program "neglects academic skill development, trains for occupations not in demand, teaches with outmoded equipment, and offers limited placement assistance." The report found that *less than half* of all students who take high school vocational education are able to use what they learned in full-time jobs following high school. As you can see in Table 2, the course utilization rates are poor in some job areas: Less than one-quarter of the men who studied communications and less than one-third of the women who studied occupational home economics were able to use what they learned after they graduated.

Unemployment among students who graduated from vocational education programs in comprehensive high schools *averages* more than 20%, and the average wage for students who do find work is less than $7.00 an hour. There are, of course, some excellent vocational education programs in some comprehensive high schools, and the next chapter will show you how to identify them. For the most part, however, it's not a good idea to count on getting a good job based on what you learn in the vocational education program in most comprehensive high schools.

2. Specialized vocational/technical (vo-tech) high schools. These are two to four-year high schools where all students major in some form of vocational education, although all receive the same fundamental academic instruction of conventional high schools.

ADVANTAGES: Many are outstanding schools. They offer far more comprehensive, in-depth training by skilled craftspeople in each trade than ordinary high schools, thus making each graduate more skilled and employable. Employers generally respect the credentials of graduates from vo-tech schools, which usually have strong job placement services and close ties with employers. Vo-tech students emerge stronger in academics as well, because students learn English, math, science, and other subjects in conjunction with their vocational education and, therefore, find these areas more interesting. In other words, they learn *applied* rather than theoretical mathematics. Student self-esteem is usually higher, because the entire administration and fac-

RATES OF HIGH SCHOOL VOCATIONAL COURSE UTILIZATION BY SUBJECT AREA

Table 2. According to the U.S. Department of Education, these are the percentages of high school graduates able to use the vocational courses they studied in high school in the jobs they eventually secured after graduating. Even the most gender-oriented education, such as construction or mechanics and repairs for men, proved of no value for more than half the students. Occupational home economics was of value to fewer than one-third of the women students.

Vocational Subject	Course Utilization Rate	
	Men	Women
Agriculture	43.6%	26.9%
Business	32.4%	65.4%
Marketing	20.9%	38.3%
Health	7.5%	78.8%
Occupational home economics	14.4%	31.5%
Construction	42.0%	0.0%
Mechanics and repairers	45.5%	35.2%
Precision production	36.0%	17.8%
Transportation	6.2%	0.0%
Technical and communications	22.1%	31.6%
Average course utilization rates	38.0%	53.0%

Source: National Assessment of Vocational Education, U.S. Department of Education.

ulty are devoted to vocational education instead of traditional academics. In comprehensive high schools, vocational education is often held in low esteem by school administrators, who tend to assign less able teachers to vocational education students than to students in the academic, college-prep curriculum. Another advantage of specialized vo-tech schools is the time and opportunity allowed to sample many trades and occupations before deciding on a specialty. The best vo-tech schools offer prevocational courses that offer students an in-depth look at "career clusters" such as agriculture, manufacturing, health, public service and other broad categories, and then examine the hundreds of specific jobs within those clusters.

DISADVANTAGES: Usually there are none in terms of educational quality. Unfortunately, there are fewer than 500 vo-tech schools across the entire United States. Most communities have none. If there's a vo-tech school in or near your community, by all means evaluate its program and look into the possibility of enrolling.

3. Cooperative education programs. There are two kinds of co-operative education programs: One is at the high school level, the other at the college level. Both offer excellent vocational education.

  a. High school cooperative education programs: These pro-grams allow students to take vocational courses at a comprehen-sive high school in the morning and immediately apply all new knowledge on the job in the afternoon at local companies that pro-vide supervision and instruction and work closely with vocational education teachers.

ADVANTAGES: Skills taught are up-to-date and immediately applica-ble in the workplace. Close ties with local industry and employers can be a big help in getting students jobs after graduation. Involve-ment of local industry also assures schools of the most modern equip-ment and continuous training for teachers.

DISADVANTAGES: The quality of the academic education offered to vocational education students is often inadequate. That's because ad-ministrators of comprehensive high schools usually hold vocational education in lower esteem than academic education. So they some-times reserve their best teachers for college-prep programs and assign less-skilled faculty to students of vocational education. These stu-dents, however, need just as many skills in reading and comprehen-sion, mathematics, analysis and problem solving and science as aca-demic track students. Unfortunately, voc-ed students usually do not get an adequate academic education in comprehensive high schools.

The lack of interest by school administrators in vocational educa-tion is evident in the small number of comprehensive high schools that have bothered establishing cooperative education programs. Only about 3% of high school students are enrolled in formal "coop" pro-grams. From your own personal point of view, another disadvantage of a high school cooperative education program is the possibility that a decision to specialize in a trade at age 16 or 17 may be premature.

You may find that, after graduating and working at your new trade for a year, you dislike it intensely. A change then, however, may be economically impossible or, at best, difficult. It will mean going back to school either to learn another trade or to get an academic degree.

b. College cooperative education programs. These provide perhaps the finest vocational education for students who are certain about their career goals. Available at about 1,000 public and private two-year and four-year colleges and universities, cooperative education programs integrate your daily college classroom studies with a part-time paying job at a local company. About three-quarters of all community colleges, technical institutes and junior colleges now participate in one or more employer-college partnership programs in which company and college cooperate closely to produce a total learning experience. Some programs rearrange the learning schedule so that students study full-time for three months, then work full-time for three months.

ADVANTAGES: This is just about the best kind of vocational education you can get! Students who do well are almost guaranteed good jobs on the "fast track" after graduation. About 40% continue working for their cooperative education employer after graduation. Another 40% find jobs in fields directly related to their cooperative education assignments. And another 15% decide to continue their education by getting their bachelor's degrees and then enrolling in graduate school programs in law, medicine, dentistry or veterinary medicine. Another tremendous advantage is that these programs allow high school students to concentrate on academics, knowing they can enroll in excellent community college vocational studies that will almost guarantee them a job. More than 800 of the finest four-year colleges and universities and 200 two-year community and junior colleges and technical institutes offer cooperative education programs in 48 states and the District of Columbia. Some of the largest corporations and government agencies are involved, including American Telephone & Telegraph Co., Duke Power Co., NASA/Goddard Space Flight Center and Walt Disney World. Among the various vocational education programs offered are agriculture and natural resources, applied arts and crafts, business, computer science, health care, home economics, technologies and vocational arts, including construction, food service, repair and maintenance occupations and trade and industrial occupations. Write for the comprehensive *Cooperative Education Un-*

dergraduate Program Directory from the National Commission for Cooperative Education, 360 Huntington Avenue, Boston, MA 02115 or call (617) 437-3778 for information. This is an indispensible guide, with listings of all colleges offering cooperative education, the courses they offer and the companies that participate.

DISADVANTAGES: There are none, except for the lack of similar programs everywhere. Instead of only 1,000 colleges, all 3,300 American colleges and universities should be offering similar programs; and instead of only 27 major corporations sponsoring these programs, there should be thousands. If you know what career interests you most and you can find a college cooperative education program near you, by all means enroll. Remember that the 20 fastest growing occupations listed by the U.S. Department of Labor (Table 1) usually require some post-high school training, and most employers in those fields prefer an associate degree.

4. "Two-plus-two" tech-prep programs. A relatively new concept in vocational education, a two-plus-two program closely coordinates the vocational education program of a comprehensive high school with vocational education at a nearby community college. The program begins in the junior year of high school and continues for four years through community college.

ADVANTAGES: Four years of comprehensive, in-depth training *and* a college associate degree give students the highest qualifications for the workplace. Because the entire program is usually organized and supervised by the faculty at the community college, a two-plus-two program assures students of superior education at the high school level. Moreover, because it is a comprehensive four-year program, high school seniors must work seriously instead of goofing off and wasting time. Failure to perform well in 12th grade, the second year of the two-plus-two program, can mean failing the entire program. In addition to extensive vocational education, community college faculty see to it that two-plus-two students receive the same academic training and learn the same skills as students in the academic track— that is, reading speed and comprehension, analytical skills, problem-solving, decision-making, computation, computer literacy, human relations and communications skills. Still another advantage is that if, for one reason or another, a student decides against pursuing a particular trade, he or she can either remain in community college and study a new trade or transfer to a four-year college and work toward a bachelor's degree. Two-plus-two programs normally have extremely active and effective job placement services, and employers eagerly recruit graduates from these programs. More than 90% of the graduates find work in the fields in which they trained, and the average starting wage is about $9 an hour.

DISADVANTAGES: There are none in terms of educational quality. Unfortunately, the two-plus-two concept is new and not yet available in most communities. If it is available in your area, sign up!

5. Community colleges. Community colleges were originally designed as two-year public academic institutions that would serve as a transition between high school and four-year colleges and universities. Most still offer a wide range of academic courses, but almost all have added vocational training programs, many of which are among the best in the United States. As previously mentioned, many offer excellent cooperative education programs that allow you to "earn while you learn." Others integrate vocational education with nearby high school programs (see "two-plus-two" tech-prep programs). Still others offer their own independent vocational education programs. Most community colleges try to specialize in only one or two areas of vocational training such as hotel and restaurant management, health care, the graphic arts or some other career cluster.

ADVANTAGES: The cost is relatively low due to their status as part of state and city university systems. Most charge less than $500 a year for tuition for a full-time program. Community colleges also offer an opportunity to combine academic studies with vocational training. So, if you feel you need to brush up on academic skills—in math or English, for example—you can do so and still learn a craft or trade. Unlike high school, you can go to school part time and maintain a job while you're continuing your education. You can take as little or as much time as you need to complete your degree. You can take as many or as few courses as you want. You can just study one course to learn a trade without signing up for a degree program. Teachers at community colleges are usually part-time professionals. That's good, because they're up to date and knowledgeable about what's happening in their fields, and they're usually in close touch with job markets. Another point about community colleges: They are usually exceptionally caring institutions that provide far more individual attention than most four-year colleges. Their name, "community," says it all and defines their role: to serve the needs of the community and its students. Most try sincerely to do just that.

DISADVANTAGES: Not all community colleges are good. Indeed, nationally, only about 60% of community college students are able to use the college vocational training they get, and unemployment among community college graduates averages 18.9%. The high rate, however, may reflect the failure of a lot of community college students to take enough courses. As you can see in Table 3, unemployment rates among community college graduates are directly related to the number of credits in the major vocational subject, as are average hourly wages earned after graduation. Unemployment among graduates with more than 30 credits was only 6.8%, but jumped to 10.6% for students with 13 to 30 credits and to 16.1% for graduates with 12 credits or less.

TABLE 3

No. of Vocational Course Credits Taken at Community College	Unemployment Rate After One Year	Avg. Hourly Starting Wage
12 credits	16.1%	$6.58
30 credits	10.6%	$7.05
50 credits	6.8%	$7.39

Source: National Assessment of Vocational Education, U.S. Department of Education.

So, the more courses you take in a particular vocation, the more likely you will be to get a good job and use your training. But it's essential for you to evaluate community college (and all other) vocational programs before enrolling. I'll show you how to do that in the next chapter. Assuming you find a good community college, and many of them are great, it really will be up to you how much you get out of it.

6. Technical institutes. Like community colleges, these are usually two-year schools, but they are highly specialized and seldom offer extensive academic programs. They expect incoming students to have a firm command of English, mathematics and basic science. Many offer cooperative education programs of the kind discussed earlier. ADVANTAGES: These institutes usually offer high quality, in-depth training by professionals who are up-to-date on technological advances and in touch with job markets. Technical institutes normally have close working ties with nearby industries and have extensive job-placement facilities for their students.

DISADVANTAGES: Again, there are very few of them across the United States, and most are usually costlier than community colleges and require more intensive study. That makes it difficult for some students to handle the work part time. Indeed, it's best to attend full time. Despite in-depth training, only about 83.5% of graduates find work—that's only two percentage points better than students trained at community colleges (see Table 5). Only about 60% of students are able to use their training on-the-job—the same "course utilization rate" as community college students. But, as with community college students, rates of postgraduation unemployment and wages for technical institute graduates are directly related to the number of credits earned in the vocational major.

TABLE 4

No. of Vocational Course Credits Taken at Technical Institute	Unemployment Rate After One Year	Avg. Hourly Starting Wage
12 credits	19.2%	$5.84
30 credits	11.6%	$6.61
50 credits	6.4%	$7.19

Source: National Assessment of Vocational Education, U.S. Department of Education.

7. Private, not-for-profit junior (two-year) colleges. These are the same as community colleges, except that they are privately operated (although not for profit). ADVANTAGES: On average, they offer much broader academic programs than community colleges and more athletic and other extracurricular activities. Many have boarding facilities for full-time resident students. The main reason for considering private junior colleges is to see whether they offer superior programs or vocational courses and job placement services that may not be available at a local community college. Many offer cooperative education studies as discussed earlier.

DISADVANTAGES: They are usually better than community colleges and cost more.

8. Private, for-profit (proprietary) trade schools. These are specialized private schools, which usually offer training in one field only, for example, auto mechanics, hair-styling or cosmetology. Most obtain their students by advertising through the media.

ADVANTAGES: Training is quick and concentrated. Students are ready for the job market in as few as two weeks, depending on the trade. In some communities, private trade schools are the only organizations that teach certain trades, such as bartending or barbering. So students may have no choice but to attend a private trade school if they want to learn such trades.

DISADVANTAGES: There are no opportunities for academic work, and all training is limited to one field. Training can be extremely poor, because teachers are paid far less than those at community colleges and technical institutes. As you can see in Table 5, unemployment among proprietary school graduates is an incredibly high 27.7%.

TABLE 5

Institution	Unemploy-ment Rate	Course Utilization Rate	Average Hourly Starting Wage
Community college	18.9%	60.6%	$6.63
Technical institute	16.5%	60.3%	$5.92
Proprietary trade school	27.7%	52.6%	$7.40

Source: National Assessment of Vocational Education, U.S. Department of Education.

Although average starting wages for proprietary school graduates are higher than those for graduates of community college and technical institutes, they do not climb substantially with seniority. Most proprietary school training is in single-level occupations such as bartending, barbering or hairstyling. Unless people in these occupations acquire their own businesses (for example, their own tavern or barber shop), their wages will remain relatively constant throughout their careers, affected perhaps only by inflation-impelled increases. Proprietary school graduates are also 13% less likely to get jobs using their vocational training than graduates from community colleges. The biggest disadvantage of proprietary schools, however, is the danger of running into unethical and criminal operators. Some operators advertise their schools on television, accept payment from would-be students then disappear with the money, only to begin again somewhere else. The beautiful school facilities you see on the television commercials may often be cleaned-up garages or beauty parlors whose owners were paid to allow their business places to be videotaped for those commercials. The tragedy of such runaway schools is that they leave many students in debt with loans to repay for education they never received. So, beware of proprietary school advertisements. The promises they make may be lies! There are so many disadvantages to proprietary schools that if there's a good alternative, it's wise to use it. If there's no choice, however—let's say the trade you want to learn is only taught by a proprietary trade school—then be certain the school is *accredited* by the National Association of Trade and Technical Schools. (See Appendix A for the U.S. Secretary of Education's listing of nationally recognized accrediting agencies and associations.) Chapter 2 will tell you more about the importance of accreditation in evaluating vocational schools. Meanwhile, keep in mind what a U.S. government study of proprietary schools had to say:

> *Our study found patterns of misrepresentation to prospective students, lack of attention to . . . standards, low (student) completion rates, and faulty use of federal financial aid programs. Three-quarters of the students admitted without a high school degree and half the students with a high school degree dropped out . . . Certificates from many proprietary schools have little reliability.*

9. Four-year colleges and universities.   Many state and private four-year colleges and universities offer extensive vocational training programs, including excellent cooperative education programs discussed earlier and listed in the directory of the National Commission for Cooperative Education. Students can enroll full time or part time and take as few or as many courses as they want or need. Like two-year community and junior colleges, you don't have to enroll in a degree-granting program when you go to a college or university. You can just go and study the courses needed to learn a trade.

ADVANTAGES: Training can be more intensive and in greater depth than at two-year colleges, and there are far more opportunities to supplement vocational training with academic courses. You can even transfer from vocational to academic education, or vice versa. Some four-year colleges may offer training in areas not covered by two-year schools. Job placement facilities may also be more extensive. Four-year colleges usually have boarding facilities for resident students and larger recreation facilities.

DISADVANTAGES: Costs are usually much higher than at two year schools.

10. Employer/union apprenticeship programs. For students with a solid high school education, these programs usually offer the best vocational education in their specialties, especially in fields such as construction, where students earn while they learn. Most programs require about 2,000 hours of supervised, on-the-job training plus related instruction either in classrooms, by correspondence or self-study. There are more than 800 types of apprenticeship programs officially recognized by the U.S. government and the 50 states. Appendix A lists the addresses of the U.S. Labor Department's Bureau of Apprenticeship and Training in each state. Check with the office in your state to make certain that any apprenticeship programs you're considering in your area are accredited.

ADVANTAGES: The pay is usually good, and students begin their training with a job already in place. Apprenticeship programs are supervised by master craftspeople and usually represent applied education at its finest.

DISADVANTAGES: There are too few programs, and all are extremely difficult to get into. Less than 2% of American high school graduates (usually sons and daughters of union members) get into such programs. Most trades don't even offer apprenticeships. About 300,000 people are enrolled in these programs in the United States today, and less than 20% are under the age of 23. The programs are mainly meant to train adults in their mid-twenties, and the competition to get in is fierce. That lets employers choose the most skilled and most mature applicants. In other words, it's not the type of training most people can ever count on getting.

11. Employer-sponsored training programs. Unlike apprenticeship programs, these programs are usually not associated with any union. They are taught by master craftspeople and company executives and usually combine on-the-job training with limited classroom training.

ADVANTAGES: As in apprenticeship programs, trainees earn while they learn, and successful completion usually assures them permanent jobs. Instructors are usually the best the company has to offer. Once again, it is "applied" education at its best. Widespread availability makes these programs outstanding opportunities for millions of workers. Here, according to a Rand Corporation study, is the percentage of workers who reported receiving their training from their employers:

TABLE 6

Job category	Men	Women
Professional and technical workers	61.7%	63.8%
Sales supervisors, representatives and clerks	40.7	29.1
Trade and craftsworkers	38.9	31.1
Office and clerical workers	37.5	33.5
Machine operators and assemblers	26.6	19.5
Transportation workers	16.9	44.9

DISADVANTAGES: There are two possible disadvantages for applicants to be careful about. The first is that some companies may offer training that is so specific that the trainee never learns to do another job and cannot transfer the skills to another company or occupation. A car assembler who only learns to install door handles won't find many job opportunities if the car plant shuts down. So, it's important that the training program be broad-based and offer *career* training as well as *job* training.

The other major disadvantage to beware of is an employer's offer to train workers in labor-short markets. Be suspicious whenever you see an advertisement that says, "Carpenters wanted. No experience necessary. Will train. . . .'' These ads usually appear when there's a housing boom, often in resort areas that attract young people with few nonrecreational skills. In their eagerness to profit from market conditions, some builders hire workers whose only experience may have been to help their parents complete do-it-yourself projects at home. The jobs offer no real training, only the opportunity to help and observe more experienced workers. The sad results are often shoddy workmanship for the builder's clients and few marketable skills for the young workers. Compared to professionals who trained as apprentices, such trainees are slow and incompetent—even those who have worked many years. Their work may be a quick means of earning money without alternative education, but it is only temporary, because every construction boom eventually ends and workers are left without jobs or real skills. Few professional construction firms in stable labor markets hire workers who have not gone through accredited apprenticeship programs. So it's as important to evaluate employer-sponsored training programs as it is to evaluate all other forms of alternative education.

Chapter 2

How to Pick the Right Career—And the Right School to Train You for It

As you saw in Chapter 1, there are many types of vocational education, each with its own advantages and disadvantages. With so many choices, how can you decide which is the right program for you?

Well first of all, where you live may limit the number of your choices, because only a few large cities such as New York or Chicago offer all programs listed in Chapter 1. Most areas only offer two or three, and isolated rural areas may only offer one program at the local high school.

No matter how many or how few programs are available, however, it's important for you to evaluate each of them carefully so that you can choose the one that is indeed *the best for you* in your area—and there is almost always one that is better than all others. That's why evaluation is so important—to make certain you pick a program that will get you started properly in a successful and happy career. Remember: *The basic purpose of vocational education is to get a job.* If a school or training program can't teach you the skills you need to get and keep a job, it's a poor school or program, and you shouldn't waste your time with either.

Looking at it from another point of view, vocational education is an investment. You're going to invest a lot of time and perhaps a lot of money. So, as with any investment, it's important to find out *in advance* what the return on your investment will be.

There are two things to determine in evaluating any vocational education or training program: educational quality and educational results. The following checklist for evaluating vocational education outlines ten factors that make up educational quality and five that measure educational results.

CHECKLIST FOR EVALUATING VOCATIONAL EDUCATION

I. EDUCATIONAL QUALITY

1. Accreditation by appropriate organization in Appendix A _____
2. Program depth (at least four courses in your field, two at advanced levels)* _____
3. Link to local vo-tech or community college program* _____
4. Links to on-the-job training programs in local industry (cooperative education) _____
5. Up-to-date classroom equipment _____
6. Strong, required academic program (minimum 2 years English, math and science)* _____
7. One-semester course on "World of Work" (resume preparation, interviews, and so on)* _____
8. Skilled faculty _____
9. Active job-placement office _____
10. Readily available performance data _____

II. EDUCATIONAL RESULTS

1. Program completion rate (at least 75%) _____
2. Test scores and/or state certification rates (at least 75% passing grades) _____
3. Training-related job placement rate (at least 80%) _____
4. Average starting wage (at least $7.30/hour) _____
5. Duration of employment (at least two years) and unemployment rate among graduates (no more than 15%) _____

*Not appropriate for private trade schools.

Use this checklist for evaluating a vocational education program. Most of the data should be available from the school's course catalog, the rest from school administrators. Here is how to use it:

I. EDUCATIONAL QUALITY

1. Accreditation. *Do not consider* a school or program that is not accredited by an appropriate independent accreditation agency. Accreditation assures you that a program or school has met *minimum* educational standards set by impartial authorities in the particular field. It also means, first and foremost, that the school clearly has stated educational goals and the methods for achieving those goals. In the case of any vocational high school or college, the goals should be to teach each student a skill and to make sure the student obtains a job practicing that skill. Without such clearly stated goals and effective methods for achieving them, no school can obtain accreditation. Every good high school and college seeks accreditation by one of the six regional accreditation associations for schools and colleges listed in Appendix A on page 131. Lack of school accreditation almost always means substandard education. Don't even bother to continue your evaluation if a school is not accredited. Carefully check that any private trade school you're considering is accredited by the National Association of Trade and Technical Schools and that its owners are approved by the Better Business Bureau and Chamber of Commerce. In some areas, some proprietary schools may be set up by con artists, eager to steal student funds. All legitimate trade schools should be accredited. Appendix A lists the names, addresses and telephone numbers of the various accreditation agencies and associations for every type of vocational education program and school. Part II on career opportunities gives the names of professional associations that also accredit specific occupational training programs. There is one possible exception to the accreditation rule: Some small companies that train their workers may not have formally accredited training programs. Nevertheless, it's important to evaluate the training they offer as best as you can. Check on the company's reputation in the community by calling the Better Business Bureau and the Chamber of Commerce and by asking employees what they think of the training they received. If you're looking at vocational schools, be certain they are accredited by one of the agencies listed in Appendix A.

2. Program depth. With some exceptions such as bartending, which is taught in a single two-week course, a program that offers fewer than four courses in most occupational areas is probably only providing superficial training, which won't teach you how to be a master craftsperson. Check on the number of advanced *second-level* and *third-level* courses, which offer specific *job* and *career* training as well as *skill* training. A course in basic welding, for example, probably isn't enough to get you a job as a welder even though it teaches you a basic skill. For a welding program to have any market value, it must have courses that show you how to weld parts and materials for *specific jobs*. Vehicle-repair companies usually don't hire "welders;" they hire welders who know how to work on vehicles. So, make sure the program has advanced "occupationally-specific" courses—and that usually means at least four courses (20 credit hours) in each area.

In terms of the "return on your investment," look at Table 7 and compare the differences among the number of courses and credit hours you take (three to five credit hours per course) to the hourly wage you will make and your chances of getting a job:

TABLE 7

No. of Credit Hours in Major	Hourly Wages*	Unemployment
12	$6.93	20.5%
30	$7.30	16.3%
45	$7.98	13.3%

* The hourly wages are *average* for *all* vocational school graduates, regardless of the type of work.
Source: National Assessment of Vocational Education, U.S. Department of Education.

In other words, the more courses you take in your major, the better chance you'll have of getting a job with higher wages. Indeed, every additional 30 credit hours in your major will increase your wages 12.2%, which is a better return on your investment than you usually can get on Wall Street. Don't consider any school that can't offer you enough credits to get a good job with good pay.

3. Ties to other vocational education institutions (for high schools only). If you're looking at a program at a comprehensive high school, be certain it has ties to a nearby vo-tech high school or community college program in the same field (see cooperative education and "two-plus-two'' programs in Chapter 1) so that you can get enough credits to get a good, high paying job.

4. Integration of theoretical and applied aspects of vocational instruction. Top-quality high school and college programs link what they teach in classrooms to on-the-job training and application. It's not enough for a school to have a small "shop." It must tie its vocational instruction to a cooperative education program (see Chapter 1) with local employers in the same field and thus link formal school training with work experience.

5. Up-to-date equipment. Although few schools or colleges can afford to replace equipment annually, good programs offer students the opportunity to work with "state of the art" equipment that they will encounter on the job. There's no point learning auto mechanics on a Model-T Ford!

6. Integration of academic skills with vocational skills (does not apply to proprietary trade schools). Every job today requires a firm knowledge of oral and written language communication skills as well as skills in computation and problem solving and a knowledge of basic principles of science and technology.* A top-quality vocational school teaches these and other academic skills along with vocational skills, because there is a direct connection between academic disciplines such as science and laboratory experiments, economics, mathematics and communication and real-life work such as accounting, agriculture, clerical and secretarial work, construction, electrical service, food service, graphic arts, health services, marketing, mechanics, metal fabrication, transportation and other occupations. Good vocational education programs have the same academic skill requirements as college prep programs. One irony of the American job market is that unemployment has been *rising* despite the increasing shortage of technically trained workers. And that's because too many U.S. schools are graduating uneducated, unskilled young people who are

---

* Leading educators agree that a basic course in Principles of Technology should explain the concepts of force, work, rate, resistance, energy, power, force transformers, momentum, energy converters, optical systems, transducers, time constants, vibrations and radiation. In evaluating any vocational education program, be certain that a Principles of Technology course is included and that it covers those topics.

unable to cope with the expanding technology of the workplace. Almost every job in modern society will require that you be able to read and write well, make logical decisions and act on the basis of complex data. That's why it's so important for you to carefully evaluate any vocational education program you're considering. As the U.S. Department of Labor explains in its *Occupational Outlook Handbook,* "The connection between high unemployment rates and low levels of education shows the importance of education in a job market that increasingly requires more training." An astounding 23 million Americans can't read, write or calculate adequately to hold a permanent job, and that number is increasing by about 5 million every 10 years. Make certain you do not join them.

7. The World of Work. Good schools now teach both academic and vocational students two courses called "The World of Work." One is a standard prevocational education course that explores a dozen or more "job clusters"—agriculture, manufacturing, health care, and so on—then explains the function of individual jobs within each cluster. The second course in "The World of Work" curriculum shows you how to look for jobs, write resumes, fill out job applications, have job interviews and handle all other details of looking for, finding and keeping a job. It also teaches basic job skills such as promptness, proper behavior and relationships on the job with coworkers, employers and clients. More employees are fired because they can't get along with others than for *any* other reason. A school that doesn't have courses on "The World of Work" is not doing a good job for its students.

8. Faculty quality. Teachers in vocational education should have worked in the trade they teach and should continually update their skills. You have a right as a consumer to ask the principal of any school or the director of vocational education whether that is indeed the case. A good school gladly will give you a list of its faculty and their credentials. If not, look for another school or program.

9. Job placement office. A hallmark of quality in all vocational education programs is an *active* job placement office with skilled *job counselors.* They're not the same as guidance counselors. Job counselors have in-depth knowledge of and *ties to* the job market. They'll study your qualifications, help you write a good resume, then personally *contact* prospective employers for you.

10. Performance information. Top-quality schools and colleges measure how well their students and graduates are doing, and they are proud to share this data with prospective students. Availability and display of performance results are thus two other educational quality hallmarks of any vocational school. Any hedging about such performance results—any failure *to be specific*—is a clear signal that the school is *inferior*. So walk away! The type of data every good vocational school proudly displays—completion rates, job placements, earnings of graduates, and so on—are discussed under "Educational Results." Any vocational school or college that says it doesn't have this data or that the information is confidential is either not truthful or incompetent. In either case, you'll be wasting your time and money by attending.

II. EDUCATIONAL RESULTS

1. Completion rate. In evaluating any vocational education program, it's important to know how many students complete the program. A high drop-out rate (more than 25%) may reflect a poor program, which is unable to sustain student interest.

2. Test scores and certification rates. A key measure of program quality is the percentage of graduates that successfully earns state certification or licensing in a field of study. If the certification rate is less than 75%, the program may either be teaching obsolete skills or may be poorly taught. Where no state certification is required, many states nevertheless require schools to administer tests of knowledge and skills in the field studied. Unfortunately, most high schools don't know how their graduates do after graduating, and that indifference is a sign of a poor-quality school. A good school knows and will gladly tell you how its students have performed on certification tests or on tests that measure competency or employability.

3. Job placements *and* the degree to which those placements are *training related*. The quality of job placement assistance is the third important element in evaluating performance results of a vocational education program. After all, if you can't get a job with the training you get, what good is it? Any school or college whose placement service can't find jobs for at least 80% of its students either has a poor placement service or is offering inferior training. Nor is it doing a good job if it places its graduates in jobs *unrelated* to their training. There's no point in learning auto mechanics at a school that can only get you a job as a dishwasher after you graduate. Again, these schools don't know how or what their graduates are doing. Good schools do.

4. Average starting wage for graduates and average wage at regular intervals thereafter.   A school that does not follow up on the effectiveness of the training it gives its students may be inferior. So, if the program director doesn't know or won't reveal these figures, try to find a better program. The *average* starting wage for graduates of a good vocational or technical school should be at least $7.30 an hour.

5. Duration of employment and unemployment among graduates of the program.   Why bother to enroll in a program whose students end up on unemployment lines? You have a right to know whether the program you sign up for is an effective one. If it isn't, don't sign up! There are many other routes to success.

Regardless of what school catalogs and school officials may say about the effectiveness of their program, it's important to protect your interests by double-checking their claims independently. Be especially careful to double-check the educational quality, educational results and accreditation of proprietary schools, that is, the private trade schools that frequently advertise in the media. The best way is to call or meet a few former students and local employers and ask them what they think of the vocational education program at the school you're considering. In the case of graduates, ask them how they're doing. Did the school get them their jobs? Has the training proved useful? Could they have succeeded without the training at school? In other words, did they get their money's worth from the school? In the case of employers, ask how well graduates from the program are doing, how far they've advanced at the company, what they're earning after one, two, five or ten years, and how long they usually last at the company. Don't put 100% faith in what the school tells you. Check out some of the school's claims yourself! If a school won't give you a list of graduates or employers, walk out. Cross them off your list. If local companies say they don't know anything about the program or if they're reluctant to discuss it or are unenthusiastic about it, there's probably something wrong. People seldom hesitate to compliment good programs, but they do hesitate to criticize bad ones for fear of lawsuits. If you run into this kind of reluctance after two calls to local companies, pick out a third one—one you'd really like to work for—and ask for an interview with a personnel representative. At the interview, simply ask what qualifications you'd need to get the job you want. Then ask where they think you could get the best training. If they fail to mention the vocational education program you were considering, you know it can't be very good and won't help you get a job at that particular company.

Preliminary Evaluations

Before going to the trouble of making an in-depth evaluation of a school or its program, you can probably save yourself a lot of time and effort by simply getting a course catalog and doing a preliminary evaluation that will allow you to eliminate the poorest schools and programs. Most school course catalogs will give you enough information to fill most of the checklist and thus help you decide if the school is good enough to warrant an in-depth evaluation. If it is, arrange to visit the school and interview the program administrators and a few teachers who can give you the answers to all the questions on the checklist. Then, if you still feel the program is a good one, double-check by contacting some local employers as suggested earlier.

Cross off your list any school without a course catalog and complete descriptions for each course—and, except for one-course trades like bartending, cross off any program that doesn't offer at least four courses in your chosen vocational area, with at least two advanced level courses or two courses that tie into advanced education at a nearby community college (tech-prep).

Selecting the "Right" Program—for You

In general, the "right" program for you is the one that will get you a good job after graduating and put you on the road to a happy and successful career. Employers simply don't hire and keep poorly trained employees. So, after deciding what type of career interests you most, go to the people you'll eventually work for and ask them about the type of education and training they either require or prefer. Then find out if it's available locally. It's also a good idea to contact trade

associations and professional organizations in the fields that interest
you. Where available, their names and addresses are listed with each
occupation in Part II on career opportunities.

As pointed out earlier, many communities in the U.S. simply don't
have outstanding vocational education facilities such as area vocational schools, two-plus-two programs, technical institutes or em-
ployee/union apprenticeship programs. That leaves most available opportunities for vocational education limited to comprehensive high
schools, most of which have inadequate vocational training programs
that will only give you a taste of knowledge without any of the in-
depth training you'll need to get a good job in the field you want to
enter. Indeed, signing up for vocational studies (or even worse, general studies) in many high schools could actually hurt your chances
of getting a job in the field you like when you graduate. That's because most comprehensive high schools spend more money on academics than on vocational education, and, as mentioned earlier, they
assign their best, highest paid teachers to students studying for academic diplomas in "the academic track." That means students studying for vocational diplomas or general diplomas might get the educational leftovers. That's tragic but true, and it's something you may
have to face and respond to appropriately if you plan to succeed in
your chosen field. By choosing the vocational track in many high
schools, you may get poor vocational and academic training—and
that's an educational combination almost guaranteed to lead to unemployment after you graduate.

The General Education Track

Even worse than the vocational track in most U.S. high schools is
the so-called "general" track, which provides the worst academic
program available in school and useless pseudo-vocational courses
such as home economics, arts and crafts, human relations and personal improvement and equally useless academic courses and per-
sonal/hobby courses, which are usually called general science, general social studies, general math and remedial English.

"The high school general-education program," says Dale Parnell,
long-time president of the American Association of Community and
Junior Colleges and one of the most respected educators in the United
States, "is the academic and vocational desert of American educa-

tion. [It] relates to nothing, leads to nothing and prepares for nothing.'' Parnell strongly believes that good education must prepare young men and women for coping with real life as ''citizens, wage earners, family members, producers, consumers and life-long learners.'' The general education programs of U.S. high schools fail utterly in this task. Indeed, most are nothing more than custodial services for nonachievers. Surely, you do not fit that description. Otherwise you would not be reading this book.

There is no way to overemphasize the importance of staying out of the general education program in your school if you're still in high school. *Avoid this program at all costs.* Any guidance counselor, teacher, school administrator or fellow student who urges you to take general education courses in high school is insulting your intelligence—and probably condemning you to a life of unemployment and poverty. General education is a dumping ground for students whom teachers don't want to bother teaching. General education is the worst disaster U.S. high schools have ever experienced. Some 42% (about 52 million) of American high school students are now enrolled in general education programs—and 63.5% *(almost two-thirds)* drop out of school. The nearly 2.2 million general education students who drop out every year account for two-thirds of all high school dropouts in the United States. What happens to them? Well, more than 37% are unemployed, and those who do find work earn an average of less than $6,000 a year—about $112 a week. Any friend who tries to convince you that general studies are fun or easy is no friend; and any guidance counselor, teacher or school administrator who says you'll be ''better off'' in general studies is lying. You'll be worse off. The U.S. Department of Education and dozens of other organizations have facts and figures to prove it. *Do not enroll in general studies* if you want to assure yourself a successful, secure future after graduating from high school. Stick to academic (college prep) or vocational programs.

''But,'' you may be asking yourself, ''why bother working so hard in the high school academic or vocational track if I can take it easy and have fun in the general education track and still go to college?''

It's true that almost all community colleges and most state colleges and universities admit students on a first-come, first-served ''open enrollment'' basis. Almost anyone can get into a community or state college or technical institute regardless of the courses they took in high school or their high school grades. But getting *into* college won't get you a good job. You'll have to get *out* of college to do that. You'll have to *graduate* from community or state college, and there simply is no way you'll succeed if you took the easy way out in high school with general studies courses and less than your best effort. That's why more than 50% of all college students never finish. They can't. They didn't get a quality high school education to do so— probably because they thought too much about college *entrance* requirements and too little about college *exit* requirements and the type of high school preparation needed to fulfill those requirements.

Most high school students have unrealistic expectations about college largely because guidance counselors only tell them about entrance requirements and seldom discuss exit requirements. A few years ago, Pennsylvania State University's James Kelly surveyed 18,000 incoming freshmen and found few that had any realistic idea about the requirements for completing their college programs. About 98% expected to earn B averages or better at college and 61% thought they'd only have to study about 20 hours a week or less. In reality, only about 10% of students at colleges such as Penn State earn B averages or better, and most students have to study at least 30 hours or more each week.

Community colleges are seldom as academically demanding as schools such as Penn State, but the expectations of high school students headed for community colleges are no less unrealistic than the Penn State students surveyed about their expectations. The point is not to let the ease of entry into college convince you not to take demanding courses at high school. You'll need that firm academic grounding to fulfill the college's *exit* or graduation requirements. So again, don't let a friend or guidance counselor talk you into taking a general studies program simply because it meets all the college entrance requirements. Over the long term, it will prove useless and the preceding statistics prove that.

Be just as careful about enrolling in vocational studies in any comprehensive high school. No matter how good the school administrators, guidance counselors and teachers say the vocational program is, make certain *you* carefully evaluate the program and the courses offered. *Most vocational education in comprehensive high schools is substandard.* Nearly 30% of all high school dropouts in the U.S. are vocational education students, that is, more than one-million vocational education students drop out every year. Remember, too, the statistics in Table 2 (Chapter 1) show how few students actually were able to use the vocational training they received in high school in their workplace after high school. I can't emphasize enough the importance of relying on your own evaluation and not that of a guidance counselor, teacher or school administrator. Let's be realistic: It's unlikely that any counselor, teacher or school administrator will tell you, "Our vocational courses are not adequate, our program is quite poor, and I don't think you'll learn enough to get a good job when you graduate." So, use the rules previously listed and the easy-to-use checklist on page 28 to do your own evaluation; talk to graduates of the program; and get the opinions of local employers. Trust nothing else.

What If There Isn't Any Good Vocational Education?

Let's say your evaluation of the high school vocational education program shows it to be mediocre or poor. What course can you take to achieve your career goals? The best answer may be to postpone your vocational education plans and take advantage of what your high school can offer—namely, a firm grounding in academics in the college prep program.

Most businesses and industries now are demanding that the men and women they hire *for all jobs* be skilled in written and verbal communication, that is, English and perhaps a foreign language such as Spanish. Employers also insist that applicants have a firm command of mathematics and basic principles of science and a good knowledge of history and social studies. That means that vocational education students must have just about the same high school academic background that students headed for four-year universities have. The importance of academics is that they teach students how to learn, and employers rank the *ability to learn as the most important skill* they seek in employees, regardless of the jobs they perform.

Language, math and science, all academic track courses, are the tools of understanding. With a broad knowledge of academics, you can read complex instructions and understand the mathematical and scientific principles of almost any trade. You can learn almost anything, and that's the type of person American industry needs today, because rapid technological advances are making many jobs obsolete. *Careers* aren't becoming obsolete but the *jobs* are. Let's say you trained to be a secretary by learning shorthand and typing. Most of that training could prove worthless in a company that replaced most of its typewriters with word processors, computers and other high-tech equipment. Word processors and computers won't eliminate secretarial *careers,* but they will eliminate *jobs* as typists and stenographers. Today's secretaries must be administrative assistants with sophisticated skills in communications and business technology. They must be able to write and speak well. The telephone is still the major link between businesses and their clients. Secretaries must have the organizational and mathematical skills needed to maintain records, provide financial data and produce and read spreadsheets, graphs and other reports. And, again, they must be technologically versatile enough to adapt to and use computers and any other new electronic equipment which is developed.

It's the same story in almost every occupation today. What used to be a relatively simple (although back-breaking) job as a building maintenance engineer (once called janitors or superintendents) now requires a keen knowledge of mathematics and electronics. That's because so many functions in new buildings—climate controls, waste disposal and so on—are electronically controlled from computer consoles. Today's maintenance engineer may have to operate the controls for a 100-story skyscraper or a complex of 1,000 or more apartments. That takes a sound education in English, math, basic science and technology.

That's why business and industry are demanding more generalists these days—men and women who have learned how to learn and how to solve problems. Someone with a firm command of written and oral communication skills, mathematics, basic science, computer technology and keyboarding can easily convert his or her job skills from stenography or typing to computer or word processing. But if that person's education was limited to shorthand and typing, he or she faces an enormous period of retraining to keep up with fast-changing technology. Similarly, someone who only knows how to shovel coal into a furnace is ill-equipped to move into maintenance engineering and regulate electronic controls in a modern building complex.

So, if you're still in high school and you have no access to good vocational education in a cooperative education program, a two-plus-two tech-prep program or at a regional vo-tech school, postpone your plans. Second-rate vocational courses and all general diploma courses will only lead to low-wage jobs, at best, and more likely to unemployment, no matter what your guidance counselor tells you. Stay out of the vocational and general tracks, and select the academic track at your high school; then plan on getting your vocational education in the best available post-high school program you can find at a community college, a technical institute, a four-year college or an apprenticeship or company training program. Almost every employer today prefers employees and craftspeople with strong academic backgrounds, whether the work is in construction, business, health care or building maintenance. Almost every area of work has gone high-tech, and workers without strong academic backgrounds will find it difficult and, in some cases, impossible to adapt.

In addition to knowing how to learn, employees list the following as some essential employability skills: reading, writing, mathematics, computer, communications, inter-personal relations, problem-solving and reasoning, business economics, personal economics and manual and perceptual skills. In cooperation with employers, community leaders and educators, the Colorado Department of Education put together a master list of "Essential Employability Skills" (Appendix B), which gives a more complete picture of what most employers seek in "the perfect employee." Use it only as a guide, and don't worry if you don't fulfill all or even most of the expectations; it's only meant to give you a more realistic picture.

Just because your high school's only outstanding courses are in the academic track doesn't mean you shouldn't take any vocational courses, even if they're mediocre. As you can see in Figure 1, even in states with the strictest graduation requirements, you'll have more than 25% of your class time available for electives. That means you can take at least 10 elective courses, and in states with even fewer academic requirements for graduation, you can take as many as 17. That will give you ample opportunity to sample vocational courses and at least get a taste of what work is like in those fields. But don't count on any *one* course to teach you enough to get you a job after high school unless it's part of a broader vo-tech, two-plus-two, tech-prep or co-operative education program.

Figure 1. A typical four-year academic curriculum in comprehensive high schools leaves a minimum of 10 elective courses that students can select from vocational education offerings. Unless a high school offers at least four courses in a specific area or ties its courses to a cooperative education program with local companies, vo-tech school or community college vocational education program, it's unlikely that such courses will teach you enough to get a job in the trade you studied after you graduate. But even a mediocre vocational education program can give you an opportunity to sample a number of different occupational areas and help you decide whether to pursue vocational education at more advanced levels.

Subject	1st Year	2nd Year	3rd Year	4th Year
English	Grammar and Composition Literary Analysis	Grammar and Composition English Literature	Composition Literary Analysis English/Amer. Lit.	Advanced Composition World Literature
Social Studies	Anthropology Ancient History	History: Ancient/ Medieval or Modern European	American History and American Govt. The Constitution	Electives
Mathematics	Three Years Required From Among the Following Courses: Algebra I, Plane & Solid Geometry, Algebra II & Trigonometry, Statistics & Probability *(1 sem.)*, Precalculus *(1 sem.)*, and Calculus			Electives
Science	Three Years Required From Among the Following Courses: Astronomy/Geology, Biology, Chemistry and Physics or Principles of Technology			Electives
Foreign Language	Three Years Required in a Single Language From Among Offerings Determined by Local Jurisdictions			Electives
Physical Education/ Health	Physical Education/ Health 9	Physical Education/ Health 10	Electives	Electives
Fine Arts	Art History or Music History	Art History or Music History	Electives	Electives

What If I Don't Know What I Want to Do?

Most young people and many older ones don't know what they want to do. Millions make one or more false career starts, and that's all right. There are five easy ways, however, to pick the right career and keep those false starts to a minimum. The first is to broaden your perspective by examining the thousands of different job opportunities waiting for you after you've obtained the right kind of education and training. Take a look at the job listings in Appendix C to get an idea of how many jobs exist. The huge number is not meant to confuse you; it's only meant to prove that there has to be one or more jobs out there that are right for you. Part II of this book will give you some details of occupations, each of which employs at least a half million or more. To get even more complete details of those jobs and others, consult the 500-page *Occupational Outlook Handbook,* which is published every two years by the U.S. Labor Department Bureau of Labor Statistics. It is available in major public libraries and school guidance offices; or you may buy a copy from the Superintendent of Documents, U.S. Government Printing Office, Washington, D.C. 20402, (202) 783-3238, or the Bureau of Labor Statistics, Publication Sales Center, 230 South Dearborn St., 9th Floor, Chicago, IL 60604, (312) 353-1880. Additional information on occupational categories and individual jobs within those categories is available from the various professional and trade associations listed under specific career opportunities in Part II and in Appendix A.

A second way to help yourself discover your own occupational interests is to use as many high school electives as possible to "taste" vocational courses in several different areas, even if your school's vocational program is a poor one. You'll at least get an idea of what type of work you'd be doing in a variety of careers. Some guidance counselors may try to discourage you from using occupationally oriented programs as a career exploration activity, but don't let that deter you. It's your life, not theirs, and you have a right to use your electives any way you wish.

If you have the opportunity, take the prevocational course called "The World of Work," described earlier in this chapter. That's the course that examines career clusters (agriculture, health care, and so on) and the variety of jobs within each. If you decide to go to a vo-tech school or postpone your vocational education until community college, take a few beginning courses in various trades to see which ones you enjoy, and then take advanced courses in those that appeal to you most.

A third way of exploring careers is to visit businesses and factories in your area and when on vacation. Many companies gladly talk to visitors and prospective job applicants about their firms and their industries. Some conduct tours on a regular basis. Even if such tours don't produce any career ambitions, you'll find them interesting and often exciting. To see tons of molten steel (or chocolate) pouring from huge vats and transformed into a thousand different shapes is a thrill for most people, regardless of whether they plan a career in that field.

A fourth effective way to pin down career ambitions is to start from a completely different direction and list your personal interests and hobbies instead of job preferences. Forget about jobs for a moment and think about the activities and interests you enjoy most: sports, music, television, science, medicine, stamp collecting—whatever they are and no matter how far they may seem from the world of work. Make a comprehensive list of those *interests*. Only then should you begin to look at the huge number of jobs from Part II that are available and see which ones would allow you to participate in the areas that interest you most. Let's look at a few examples.

Take the sports and recreation industry. You don't have to be an athlete to have an important job in the sports world. As in any other industry, it's the behind-the-scenes office administrators and personnel who keep the sports world functioning smoothly: in team offices, stadium and arena management firms, public relations and advertising firms, catering firms and personal agents' offices. For every athlete on the field or in the arena, there are dozens of administrative and clerical workers in team offices handling promotion, travel arrangements, contracts, endorsements, guest appearances and many other behind-the-scenes activities that are as important to the sports world as the games and players themselves. And that's true for every sport. In addition, every sport needs huge staffs to operate stadiums and arenas and run the concessions; and they need aides in the locker rooms and training camps. They need tradespeople—carpenters, electricians, painters, plumbers, millwrights, groundskeepers—to prepare the stadiums and arenas for the different events.

The same holds true in every area of show business, whether it's the opera and classical concert stage, rock-and-roll music or a Broadway theater. An army of administrative and clerical personnel must prepare all the appearance and travel schedules and arrangements, and just as many carpenters, electricians and other craftspeople are needed to build and tear down sets, set up the complex electrical connections for cameras, microphones and loudspeakers and prepare arenas and stages for performers. Few are performers or have any musical or acting talent, but they're as much a part of show business and participate in it as actively as any performing star.

Every industry needs most of the skills listed under career opportunities in Part II, and the best way to assure yourself a happy and successful career is to apply your skills and training in an area you enjoy most. You don't have to limit yourself to traditional areas. Just because you're good at carpentry or electrical installations doesn't mean you have to work in construction or home renovations unless you want to. You can sell your skills anywhere—at the Metropolitan Opera House, on the Broadway stage, at NBC-TV, or in Hollywood, or you can travel with your favorite rock-and-roll band.

And just as every TV station, theater, concert hall and sports arena needs carpenters, electricians, secretaries and other behind-the-scenes professionals, so does every hospital and newspaper and every other organization you can think of, including Congress and the White House. Every doctor, lawyer, architect, governor, senator, vice president and president needs a secretary, often more than one, and clerical staffs. So when considering what you want to do, don't limit yourself to traditional jobs if they don't interest you. Define your interests first, then match your skills to those interests. For example, just because you're a clerical worker doesn't mean you have to work for an insurance company if insurance doesn't interest you. Filling out job applications at a Hollywood studio or New York City publishing company is no different from filling them out elsewhere. So pick the businesses you enjoy the most. In every area of work, there are more "stars" behind-the-scenes than there are on stage.

The same principle holds true in less visible fields. Let's say you love science or medicine but don't want to go through years of study needed to be a scientist or doctor. Again, there are thousands of administrative support opportunities in hospitals, laboratories, pharmaceutical firms and government agencies involved in science and medicine. If law interests you but you don't want to spend seven years studying to become a lawyer, the huge court systems at city, state and federal levels all need clerks, secretaries, paralegals, carpenters, plumbers, electricians, maintenance personnel, security guards and a host of other support personnel. Most of the people that keep the court house doors open are not judges and lawyers.

Remember that if you work in a field you love, you'll do a better job and be more successful at it. Don't forget that your hobbies also can provide job opportunities. There are many jobs in stores that sell stamps to stamp collectors, coins to coin collectors, books to book lovers and diamonds to diamond lovers.

Finally, a fifth way of helping you choose the right career is to pick the type of people you'd most like to be with perhaps as much as eight hours a day, five days a week, 50 weeks a year. You'd better be with people you like; otherwise you'll wind up miserable, no matter how interesting the job. Let's say you like children. Well, again, that same army of administrative support personnel and craftspeople is needed in schools, pediatric hospitals and children's institutions. If you prefer a more scholarly world, universities and colleges offer many jobs for secretaries, clerks, laboratory technicians, maintenance staffs, craftspeople, security personnel and others. So here again, the principle of picking the right career is to choose the world in which you want to work and adapt your skills to that world. Pick your own world—even if it's in the circus—rather than letting the world pick you.

What If I Have No Skills?

That's what vocational education is all about—to teach you skills. First, get that command of academics discussed earlier. Next, pin down your interests. Then, look at the types of jobs available under each area of interest. Finally, visit a company involved in that area of interest for a first-hand look at available jobs. You'll almost certainly find one and probably more that you'd like to do and could be good at. Then, it's simply a question of learning the particular craft, either at the appropriate vocational school or perhaps at the job itself in a company training program.

What If I Dropped Out of School?

If you dropped out of school, it's easy to catch up. Every state offers a High School Equivalency Testing Program for adults who have not completed a formal high school program. Usually called GED tests (for General Educational Development), they are given over a two-day period. There are five tests, each two-hours long. Test 1 measures spelling, punctuation and grammar skills and the ability to organize ideas in clear, correct sentences. Test 2 measures understanding of social studies, and asks for the interpretation of a series of passages dealing with social, political, economic and cultural problems. Test 3 on the natural sciences offers a series of passages about high school science and asks questions that test your ability to understand and interpret each passage. Test 4 deals with the understanding of literature and asks for an interpretation of a selection of poetry and prose. Test 5 tests abilities in mathematics and covers ratios, percents, decimals, fractions, measurement, graphs, plane geometry and algebra.

To pass and receive a high school diploma, you must get a minimum passing score of 35 (out of 100) on each test but earn a total score of 225 for all five, or an average score of 45 per test.

The most difficult tests for people who have been out of school for a while are tests 1 and 5, but it's easy to prepare for those and the other three in adult education classes which are offered (usually free) in many public schools and community colleges to prepare students for the GEDs. Call the principal of the local public high school for information about the courses in your area. Also helpful are some of the various GED home study books available in major bookstores. Four of the best and most popular are:

1. *Barron's How to Prepare for the High School Equivalency Examination,* Barron's Educational Series, Inc., New York
2. *High School Certification through the GED Tests,* Holt, Rinehart and Winston, Inc., New York
3. *High School Equivalency Diploma Tests,* Arco Publishing Co., New York
4. *How to Pass High School Equivalency Examination,* Cowles Education Corporation, New York

After you've completed studying, contact the education department of your state for dates and locations of the tests, and, once you've passed them, you can go to almost any college to study a trade, brush up on academics and even learn how to own and operate your own business. The only disadvantage to a GED is that it does not qualify you for a military career. The U.S. Armed Services require an actual high school diploma obtained by attending four years of high school. So, if you dropped out of high school without graduating and you're interested in the military, contact the principal of your local high school and get information about reenrollment.

PART II

*Career Opportunities—
And How to Find Them*

Chapter 3

Help Wanted: 14 Million Needed

This chapter gives brief descriptions of the many occupations open to serious, motivated men and women who don't want to go to a four-year college or university. Each listing includes the vocational education and training required. Some jobs don't even require a high school diploma; others demand an associate degree from community or junior college or a technical institute. Most jobs fall somewhere in between. If formal training is required, you'll find the appropriate agencies to contact to make sure you attend an accredited school or program for that occupation. Where no specialized accreditation agency is listed, use the accreditation organizations for schools and colleges and for trade schools to check (see Appendix A). Contacting the appropriate organizations is simple: either call or send a postcard. You can send the same message to each organization. Just say, "Please send me all available information on careers and training in (fill in the career or careers that interest you)." Then legibly write your name and address. There's no need to make it complicated or write formal letters.

Under each occupation, you'll find the pay range for beginning and experienced workers, but they represent national averages. Pay scales may vary widely from region to region as you can see from Table 8, which lists average annual salaries by state in 1989, according to the U.S. Department of Labor. Although actual salary averages may have changed slightly since then, their relationships to each other and to the national average have not. Use the factor for your state to estimate earnings in your area in the occupations that interest you most. Simply multiply the salary figures for each occupation by the factor for your state to get an approximate idea of what you'd be paid for that work in your state. For example, you'll find that average earnings for agricultural jobs are $238 a week across the U.S. If, however, you live in Alabama, where salaries are below the national average, you'd have to multiply those figures by the factor for Alabama in Figure 5,—namely .87. That means that agricultural workers in Alabama can probably only count on earning $207 a week (.87 ×

Table 8.   Average annual salaries in the United States and each state in 1989, according to the U.S. Department of Labor Bureau of Labor Statistics. Next to each salary figure is a comparison with the national average. Use that figure as a factor with which to multiply the national average salary for the occupations that interest you most in Part II to obtain the probable average income for that work in your state. Even if actual average salaries have risen or fallen since 1989, the relationship of state averages to the national average has probably remained relatively unchanged.

State	Average Annual Pay (1989)	Relation to National Average
UNITED STATES	$22,567	—
Alabama	19,593	.87
Alaska	29,704	1.30
Arizona	20,808	.92
Arkansas	17,418	.77
California	24,921	1.10
Colorado	21,940	.97
Connecticut	27,500	1.20
Delaware	23,268	1.03
District of Columbia	32,106	1.40
Florida	20,072	.89
Georgia	21,071	.93
Hawaii	21,624	.96
Idaho	18,146	.80
Illinois	24,211	1.07
Indiana	20,931	.93
Iowa	18,420	.82
Kansas	19,474	.86
Kentucky	19,001	.84
Louisiana	19,750	.88
Maine	19,202	.85
Maryland	23,466	1.04
Massachusetts	25,233	1.12
Michigan	24,853	1.10
Minnesota	25,155	.98
Mississippi	17,047	.76
Missouri	20,899	.93

State	Average Annual Pay (1989)	Relation to National Average
Montana	17,244	.76
Nebraska	17,694	.78
Nevada	21,342	.95
New Hampshire	21,551	.95
New Jersey	26,780	1.19
New Mexico	18,677	.83
New York	27,303	1.21
North Carolina	19,320	.86
North Dakota	16,932	.75
Ohio	21,986	.97
Oklahoma	19,530	.87
Oregon	20,303	.90
Pennsylvania	22,312	.99
Rhode Island	21,128	.94
South Carolina	18,797	.83
South Dakota	15,810	.70
Tennessee	19,712	.87
Texas	21,740	.96
Utah	19,362	.86
Vermont	19,497	.86
Virginia	21,879	.97
Washington	21,617	.96
West Virginia	19,789	.88
Wisconsin	20,204	.90
Wyoming	19,230	.85

$238). In addition to the jobs and average salaries listed, Appendix C lists the median weekly salaries of full-time workers by job and gender.

As you explore each occupation, remember that most listed occupations also offer management and ownership opportunities once you've acquired enough experience. So don't interpret *salary ranges* as limits on potential *earnings* for each job. Beginning workers in animal care facilities may earn only minimum wage, but owners often earn $50,000 to $100,000 a year. A security guard may start at minimum wage but can earn many thousands of dollars more as an owner of a security agency guarding scores of homes and businesses.

The job descriptions are brief and are only meant to give you an idea of what you'd be doing if you decided to follow a career in that particular line of work. Occupation listings are limited to those employing at least 500,000 people. For more complete details of work in these and many other jobs, get the *Occupational Outlook Handbook*. You can also get more details about each occupation by writing to the trade and professional associations listed under many of the career areas and to leading corporations in each field. Where no trade association is listed under a specific occupation, check in Appendix A on pages 131–135 in the U.S. Department of Education's list of "Nationally Recognized Accrediting Agencies and Associations."

Career Opportunities

AGRICULTURE

If you love the outdoors, agriculture offers a wide variety of jobs in animal care, farming, forestry, conservation, groundskeeping, nursery work and fishing and hunting.

Animal care

Feed, water, groom, exercise and train animals of all kinds in a variety of settings—ranches, farms, wildlife refuges and fisheries operated by the U.S. Fish & Wildlife Service (Department of Interior), zoos, circuses, amusement and theme parks, pounds, laboratories, animal hospitals, aquariums, kennels, stables and so on. Clean and repair animal quarters, cages, pens and tanks. Work may include careful record keeping, transporting animals and treating sick animals. All training is on-the-job, although some experience with animals (4-H Clubs, for example) preferred. Must demonstrate love for and ability to get along with animals. Salaries range from $7,000 to about $18,000 after five years. Management jobs paying up to $20,000 require a high school diploma with a solid background in math, biology and other sciences plus a community college associate degree or bachelor of science degree from a four-year college or university in animal sciences such as animal hospital technology, animal husbandry or veterinary medicine.

Farm work
Planting, cultivating, harvesting and storing crops, operating and maintaining farm machinery, tending livestock and poultry, and hauling produce, livestock or poultry to market. No schooling is required. All training is on-the-job. Pay is minimum wage permitted by state and federal laws. Work is seasonal, but workers may be laid off or hired on a day-to-day basis. There is no job security or benefits, but farm work has value as training for eventual ownership of your own farm.

Farm management
Supervise planting, harvesting maintenance and other farm operations. A highly technical profession requiring extensive skills and at least a community college associate degree (preferably a four-year college bachelor's degree) in horticulture, crop and fruit science, soil science, dairy science, animal science, farm personnel management or agricultural economics, business and finance. Farm management is as complex as managing any company in any other industry and requires a strong background in high school mathematics and science. Pay at large private or corporation farms and ranches ranges from $15,000 to start to as much as $30,000 after five to 10 years. For more career information contact your local county Agricultural Extension Service. For information about certification as an accredited farm manager, contact the American Society of Farm Managers and Rural Appraisers, 950 South Cherry Street, Denver, CO 80222. For information on agricultural education, contact your state university, which has a "land grant college" that usually provides the best agricultural education in the state at the lowest cost.

Forestry management and conservation
Planning, development, maintenance and protection of forests and woodlands, planting and raising seedlings, pest and disease control and soil conservation (control of soil erosion and leaching) for lumber companies, pulp and paper companies and the U.S. National Forest Service (Department of Agriculture) and National Park Service (Department of Interior). Although a bachelor's degree from a four-year college or university is usually required, some companies will hire applicants with a community college associate degree in forestry,

agronomy or soil sciences. Pay ranges from $12,000 to $16,000 to start and can reach $30,000 after 10 years.

Timber cutting and logging

There are almost two-dozen specialized tasks in timber cutting and logging, including site clearing and cutting, trimming, grading, and hauling trees for major lumber companies, pulp and paper companies and logging contractors who hire out to big corporations to fill seasonal demands. Work is seasonal. All training on the job is given by more experienced workers. No experience needed to start, but strength and physical fitness are essential along with maturity and the ability to work with others as a team in an extremely hazardous occupation. Average pay is $17,400 a year, with newcomers starting at less than $10,000 a year and skilled workers with seniority earning as much as $25,000. For more career information contact the school of forestry at your state land grant college or write to the Northeastern Loggers Association, P.O. Box 69, Old Forge, NY 13420; the Pacific Logging Congress, 4494 River Road North, Salem, OR 97303 and the Timber Producers Association of Michigan and Wisconsin, P.O. Box 39, Tomahawk, WI 54487.

Groundskeeping and gardening, caretaking

Maintenance of public or private property with hand and power tools. Mowing, trimming, planting, watering, fertilizing, digging, raking, sweeping, landscaping, building maintenance, pool maintenance, animal care and snow removal. Both full-time and part-time jobs are available, but they are seasonal, except in warm weather climates. Pay averages $7 per hour. Supervisory jobs at public parks and gardens, major resorts and amusement parks and some large private estates usually require some high school or community college courses in horticulture and landscape architecture. Pay at supervisory level is $14,000 to $23,000 a year. Ownership of landscape maintenance firms can produce an annual net income of up to $40,000 or more.

Nursery workers

Planting, cultivating, harvesting and transplanting trees, shrubs and plants; landscaping client properties. Seasonal, except in warm climates. Pay is minimum wage. Supervisors, with some background in horticulture, plant and insect science and landscape architecture, can earn from $14,000 to more than $20,000, and nursery owners can earn far more.

Fishing and "outfitting"

Catching fish with nets, seines and lines on board ocean-going fishing vessels; cleaning and repairing equipment. Most companies are small, privately owned firms alongside the wharfs at fishing ports. Outfitters, mostly based in western and New England cities, lead tourists on camping expeditions into the wilderness to fish, hunt or simply hike and camp. Work is seasonal. Pay is usually minimum wage, although earnings for fishers may depend on sharing profits from the catch, while outfitters depend heavily on tips. Ownership of a fishing boat or of an outfitting company can increase earnings substantially, although the seasonal nature of the work and economic conditions make this an insecure occupational area.

ARTS AND CRAFTS

Design

If you're creative, imaginative, have an eye for form and color and are a gifted artist, the opportunities in design are endless. Advancement is only limited by your talent, training, imagination and interest. About 40% of designers are self-employed. Most designers specialize in one of seven areas: industrial design, package design, textile design, apparel design, set and display design, interior design and floral design. Except for floral design, which you can learn on-the-job or by taking a one-semester course at a community college or trade school, almost all jobs in design require a minimum of two-years study at a technical institute or community college. Write to the National Association of Schools of Art and Design, 11250 Roger Bacon Drive, Reston, VA 22090 for a list of the more than 140 accredited colleges and institutes in the art and design field. Don't consider a school that is not on their list. Except for floral designers, designer salaries range from $11,000 to $50,000 a year. Self-employed designers can earn far more. The career opportunities available in design follow.

Industrial design. Create and draw designs for every conceivable manufactured product, except apparel, textiles, packaging products, stage sets and buildings. Design cars, home appliances, computers, toys, machinery, medical instruments, office supplies, furniture, sporting goods and other products that must first be in blueprint form before they can be manufactured. Virtually every manufacturer needs industrial designers. It's simply a question of picking the product area that interests you most. Industrial design requires a high school diploma with a strong background in drafting and art and at least a certificate or associate degree in the field from a technical institute, art institute or community college. Many companies and industrial design firms require a four-year college degree. Some require a mechanical engineering degree as well, because industrial designers must have a knowledge of mechanical drawing and computerized design in order to produce all the manufacturing specifications for the products they create. They're not just artists; they often are drafters and engineers and many have graduate degrees. Starting salaries range from $15,000 to $20,000 and may be as high as $25,000 for applicants with impressive educational credentials and design portfolios. Average pay for industrial designers is more than $30,000 a year, and experienced designers can earn $50,000 a year or more, although industry "superstars," with their own design firms, can earn more than $100,000 a year. Write to Industrial Designers Society of America, 1142 E. Walker Road, Great Falls, VA 22066 for information on careers and educational programs in industrial design.

Package design.   Design boxes, cans, bottles, and plastic packages and their labels and wrappings. Must have in-depth knowledge of every type of paper, paperboard, metal, plastic and composite material and the structural strength of each, whether it can or should be extruded or molded and which shape is most appropriate for the product it must contain. Just look at the enormous variety of packaging in a drug store or supermarket to get an idea of how complex package design is and why many package designers are graduates of four-year colleges and engineering schools. As in industrial design, however, two years at an art or technical institute is sometimes enough to get started; but a knowledge of mechanical drawing and computerized design is essential. Average income is about $25,000 a year—about $10,000 to start and $35,000 for experienced designers. Again, there's almost no limit to the earnings of design "superstars" and owners of their own design firms.

Textile designers. Design fabrics for garments, upholstery, rugs, draperies and every other type of textile product. Must have thorough knowledge of textiles, fabric construction and fashion trends. Textile manufacturers are the major employers, and pay is about the same as for package designers. Although a bachelor of fine arts degree is a definite plus, there are ample opportunities for designers with an impressive portfolio and a two-year associate degree or certificate in textile or fashion design from a community college or technical institute. For more career information and a list of accredited schools and colleges, write to American Apparel Manufacturers Association, 2500 Wilson Blvd., Arlington, VA 22201.

Fashion designer. Design coats, suits, dresses, hats, handbags, shoes, gloves, jewelry, underwear and other apparel for manufacturers and department and specialty stores. Strong portfolio of original designs required plus high school diploma (solid background in art and fashion design) and at least a certificate or associate degree in fashion design from a two-year technical institute or community college. Many fashion designers have four-year university degrees and even graduate degrees in art, although some are so gifted they were able to go right to work after high school with no college training at all. It's important to have studied garment construction, however, along with fashion design and sketching. Salaries range from $15,000 to $35,000, although there's almost no limit to earnings of top high-fashion designers who work for the most exclusive couturiers or for their own clientele. Other high earners in the field are the costume designers who work for theater, opera, television and movie production companies. For information on careers and education, write to the American Apparel Manufacturers Association, 2500 Wilson Blvd., Arlington, VA 22201.

Interior design. Plan and furnish the interiors of private homes, buildings and commercial establishments such as offices, restaurants, hotels and theaters. Draw designs for use of interior space; coordinate colors; select furniture, floor coverings and draperies; design lighting and architectural accents. Must have knowledge of architectural drawing. Although many interior designers work on salary ($15,000 to $30,000) for furniture, home furnishings and department stores, builders, hotel chains and major resorts, the majority are self-employed and have their own clientele, which regularly redecorates their current homes as well as newly acquired residences. Earnings for independent interior designers are limited only by the number and wealth of clients and a willingness to work hard and to find and get along with new clients. Although training varies, the minimum acceptable is a certificate or associate degree in interior design from a technical institute or community college. For career information, write the American Society for Interior Designers, 1430 Broadway, New York, NY 10018.

Set and display design.   Design stage sets for movies, television and theater, store displays in windows and on selling floors and advertising sets. In addition to artistic skills, set and display design requires a thorough knowledge of architecture and structural materials and the ability to draw rooms, buildings or street scenes in a manner that would *appear* to be realistic from the spectator's point of view at a play, in a movie theater, through a television screen or from the sidewalk looking into store windows. Many TV and movie sets that appear true to life are actually miniatures only inches wide. The camera makes them look life-size, and the set designer must know how to create such special effects. That means taking courses in set design at art school. Opportunities in set design range from small theaters and local television stations to Broadway theaters, major networks, Hollywood film studios, independent film and TV producers and advertising agencies. Starting pay for design assistants is seldom more than $12,000, but there's no limit to the income of an experienced set designer, whose name is featured among the credits for major theater, film and TV productions. Display designers earn between $15,000 and $40,000 depending on the size of the department store or advertising agency and whether it is in a small town or major city. Minimum educational requirements are an associate degree or certificate in set or display design from a technical institute or community college. Most theaters and studios, however, prefer a four-year bachelor of arts degree in theater production and set design.

Floral design.   Arrange flowers in retail flower shops or at hotels, restaurants, banquet halls and other institutional consumers. No high school diploma required, and most florists will train workers on the job. A certificate in floral design from a trade or technical school is a plus, and a degree in floriculture and floristry from a community college is preferred for entry into management or ownership where knowledge of flower marketing and shop management is needed. Salaries range from $9,000 to start to $15,000 for experienced designers. Managers' salaries average $14,000, while self-employed floral designers and shop owners average more than $30,000. The Society of American Florists (1601 Duke Street, Alexandria, VA 22314) has more career information. Write also to the Education Division, Florist Transworld Delivery, 29200 Northwest Highway, Southfield, MI 48036.

Photography and camera work
Here are two exciting areas—with vast, expanding, high-paying job opportunities that don't require a high school diploma or college degree. Both, however, require a deep interest, a lot of imagination, creativity, sense of timing and in-depth technical knowledge acquired either in school or on your own. About 1,000 colleges and vo-tech schools offer courses in photography and camera work, but both are areas where on-the-job training is the primary source of education. The two areas are quite separate, and each has its own specialties.

Photography involves still shots in portrait, fashion, advertising, industrial, special events, scientific, news or fine arts photography. Photographers may be salaried or work on their own as freelancers; some subcontract their laboratory work, others do their own. Advertising and industrial photographers take pictures of every imaginable person, place or thing—buildings, landscapes, animals, manufactured products, machinery, company executives and personnel for posters, catalogs, shareholders' annual reports, newspapers, magazines, educational presentations and advertising. Job opportunities exist with private photo studios, major corporations, advertising and public relations firms, book publishers, educational institutions and government at every level. Scientific photographers work for educational institutions, corporations in the scientific products and pharmaceutical fields and federal government agencies dealing with scientific research and health. News photographers work for newspapers, magazines, public relations and advertising firms, major corporations and government agencies. Most photographers spend two to three years in on-the-job training as photographers' assistants learning laboratory work, electrical work and camera and lighting set-ups. Starting pay is usually between $15,000 and $30,000 a year, but quickly moves into the $25,000-to-$35,000 range as you begin taking over routine photographic work yourself. After five to ten years, top-notch photographers can earn upwards of $40,000 a year. Self-employed photographers can earn much more. Some portrait photographers for Hollywood stars and other famous people earn more than $100,000 a year. For more information write to Professional Photographers of America, 1090 Executive Way, Des Plaines, IL 60018, and the American Society of Magazine Photographers, 419 Park Avenue South, New York, NY 10016.

Camera operators need no formal schooling, but, as in photography, they must show a deep interest and acquired knowledge on their own. Training is on the job as a first and second assistant to a camera operator setting up equipment and electrical gear. Salaries are similar to those of photographers. Skilled camera operators, either free lance or salaried, earn more than $50,000 a year and are in constant demand. Remember: They are the "eyes" of every film producer and the only way producers and directors can convey what they see to the public. (Don't confuse camera operators with projectionists, who set up and operate projection and sound equipment in movie theaters and are only paid by the hour, usually not more than $8. Like theater lighting projectionists, however, pay varies according to geographic area and whether or not the trade is unionized in that area.)

Art photography
This is a highly specialized field with few opportunities for any but the most artistically talented. Most art photographers are graduates of fine arts colleges or universities and have simply chosen photography as their medium instead of canvas and paints or stone and chisel. Most art photographers rely on some other form of photography for a living.

Fine arts
The fine arts include drawing, painting, sculpture, ceramics and a wide variety of crafts ranging from weaving to model making and from wood carving to glass blowing. Although no diplomas or college degrees are required, anyone considering the fine arts must demonstrate talent and have a portfolio to prove it. Most fine artists study art at four-year art schools or liberal arts colleges and universities,

and many have graduate degrees. Job opportunities are limitless, although most are in commercial or graphic art as illustrators for magazines, books, newspapers, greeting cards, album covers, posters and films. Advertising agencies and the entertainment industry need artists to draw story boards, which tell a story in a series of pictures before the scenes are acted out. Other opportunities exist in the cartoon and comic strip fields as well as in film animation. Salaries range from $12,000 to $40,000, although earnings reach far higher for self-employed "superstars" in the trade. The Graphic Artists Guild (11 West 20th Street, New York, NY 10011) has more information about the graphic arts. If you're interested in being an illustrator, write to The Society of Illustrators, 128 East 63rd Street, New York, NY 10021.

Outside the commercial and graphic arts fields, fine artists may create original works for sale to the public through galleries and other retail outlets. Other opportunities exist in the decorative arts field in major cities and in the souvenir art field in major resort areas where many tourists prefer paintings of the sights they've seen to ordinary snapshots. In the decorative arts, there are many decorative arts houses in major cities that hire artists to create or reproduce paintings to size, that is, to fit a particular client's wall space in various areas of an apartment or house.

There are fewer opportunities for sculptors than painters. Most opportunities for three-dimensional art are in architecture, the production of public monuments, religious sculptures and mortuary art and existing statuary restoration. Artists' earnings are unpredictable and vary widely, from "starvation" wages to millions.

BUSINESS ADMINISTRATION

This broad category of clerical operations critical to virtually every business and organization includes adjusters (customer complaints), account and bill collectors, advertising clerks (taking orders), bank tellers, billing clerks, bookkeepers, brokerage clerks (Wall Street firms), cashiers, computer operators, court clerks (see Government Service), credit checkers and loan authorizers, customer service representatives (telephone companies, other utilities and businesses), data entry clerks, company dispatchers (scheduling, dispatching workers), emergency dispatchers (police, fire, ambulance—see Government Service), file clerks, general office clerks, hotel desk clerks and cashiers (see Hospitality), insurance claims and policy processing clerks, mail clerks, messengers, meter readers, order clerks, payroll clerks, production planning clerks, real estate clerks, reception and information clerks, reservation and travel clerks, statistical clerks, traffic clerks (shipping, receiving and inventory), travel ticket agents, secretarial positions, stenographers, telephone operators, typists and word processor operators and many others.

Clerical support is essential to every organization in this country—every school, every corporation and business and every government agency—even the White House. Clerks in every organization are responsible for handling the data that makes that organization function. They receive, classify, store (in computers or file cabinets), distribute and retrieve all essential information and paperwork flowing through the organization. The paper they handle may be cash in the case of bank tellers, insurance claims in that industry, purchase orders, invoices and incoming and outgoing checks in every organization and airline tickets and reservation confirmations in the travel business. In addition to handling data, clerks are often "the front line" in an organization's dealings with clients and the public, greeting them over the telephone or in the reception area and either handling client needs themselves or referring clients to the right people or departments. Clerks are the heart of almost every organization, and no organization can function without their skills.

Technological advances, however, have muddied the waters of business administration, and many jobs have been eliminated by new machines and electronic devices. The copier alone has put thousands of typists out of work. The personal computer has eliminated and will continue to eliminate thousands of other clerical jobs; and automatic, computerized telephone answering devices are putting operators out of work. But the elimination of a *job* does not necessarily mean the elimination of a *career*, especially in business administration. That is why those entering this career must now get a broader education than many high schools offer. That is why it's essential to evaluate business education courses very carefully. It's essential to check with local employers and graduates of any business education program to determine its value. At most high schools, it will prove far more worthwhile to take good academic courses in English composition and writing skills than to learn obsolete vocational skills that no employer can use. Remember the U.S. government study of vocational education in Chapter 1 (see Table 2), showing that more than half the students who take vocational courses in high school are unable to use what they learn on the job. That's because so many high schools are behind the times and teach skills that became obsolete years ago.

Unless your high school has a strong program in business administration, the best way to a successful career in this field is to take a strong academic program in high school and a strong business administration program at a community college. Anyone planning a career in business administration needs a broad background in technology, and that means high school math, science and English and the study of computers and electronic office equipment either in high school or community college or both. An associate degree in business administration from a community college will help you get a better job and prepare you for a career in which you can shift easily from one job function to another as technology eliminates some jobs but creates others.

Depending on their educational background, people in the clerical field can earn anywhere from $9,000 a year to salaries of $40,000 at the office management level. The upper end of the pay range depends on these factors: education, experience, breadth of technological understanding, ability to handle responsibilities, average salaries in the industry and the standing of the particular company within the industry.

The U.S. government starts office clerks at about $11,500 a year if they are high school graduates and have had six months experience. General office clerks in the U.S. government earn an average of $17,300 a year, while secretaries earn an average of about $19,000. Secretarial salaries in private industry are higher, usually $22,000 on average and ranging above $30,000, depending on responsibilities. Clerical supervisors earn up to $45,000 a year. For career information in most areas of clerical work, contact Professional Secretaries International, 301 East Armour Blvd., Kansas City, MO 64111; the National Association of Legal Secretaries, 2250 East 73rd Street, Tulsa, OK 74136; and the American Association of Independent Colleges and Schools, 1 Dupont Circle NW, Washington, DC 20036. The last organization has brochures on careers in almost all clerical functions.

CONSTRUCTION TRADES

As in most categories in this section, construction offers endless opportunities to work for oneself, for small or large contractors, for major corporations and organizations, and for municipal, county, state or federal government agencies. Even the White House needs carpenters and plumbers. The construction trades offer opportunities in the city or country building, renovating, repairing and maintaining small structures and large ones, including the world's tallest skyscrapers. Crafts include bricklaying, carpentry, carpet installation, drywall installation and finishing, electric installation, glazing (glass installation), insulation installation, painting and wallpaper hanging, plastering, plumbing and pipefitting, roofing, stone, cement and concrete masonry, structural and reinforcing metal work (erecting steel frameworks of bridges and buildings), tile setting, paving, heavy equipment operations, road and bridge building, and excavation and loading machine operations. In all areas, a high school diploma is not required, but it is certainly a plus. Today's technology requires a solid background in reading, writing, mathematics and science. The ability to solve problems quickly also is essential. Training can be on the job, but the best training is in apprenticeship programs that last anywhere from two to five years depending on the trade, and include both on-the-job and classroom instruction in subjects such as blueprint reading, layout work, sketching, mathematics, tool and materials technology and safety. For general information about apprenticeship programs in the construction trades write to any of the following:

> Associated Builders and Contractors, 729 15th Street NW, Washington, DC 20005
> Associated General Contractors of America, 1957 E Street NW, Washington, DC 20006
> Home Builders Institute, Educational Division of National Association of Home Builders, 15th and M Streets NW, Washington, DC 20005

For information on apprenticeship programs and careers in specific trades, write to any of the organizations that follow, but also look in Appendix A for the office of the U.S. Department of Labor Bureau of Apprenticeship and Training in your state to check that any local apprenticeship program in your area has been approved by the government and industry.

Bricklaying and stone masonry. International Union of Bricklayers and Allied Craftsmen, International Masonry Institute Apprenticeship and Training, 815 15th Street NW, Washington, DC

20005; Brick Institute of America, 11490 Commerce Park Drive, Reston, VA 22091.

Carpentry, ceiling tile installation, and accoustical carpentry. United Brotherhood of Carpenters and Joiners, 101 Constitution Avenue NW, Washington, DC 20001.

Carpet installation. Floor Covering Installation Contractors Assocation, P.O. Box 2048, Dalton, GA 30722.

Concrete masons and terrazzo workers. International Union of Bricklayers and Allied Craftsmen (see also *Bricklaying and stone masonry*); Operative Plasterers and Cement Masons' International Association of the United States and Canada, 1125 17th Street NW, Washington, DC 20036; National Terrazzo and Mosaic Association, 3166 Des Plaines Avenue, Des Plaines, IL 60018.

Construction and building inspectors. International Conference of Building Officials, 5630 South Workman Mill Road, Whittier, CA 90601; Building Officials and Code Administrators International, Inc., 4051 West Flossmoor Road, Country Club Hills, IL 60478; American Society of Home Inspectors, 3299 K Street NW, Washington, D.C. 20007; International Association of Plumbing and Mechanical Inspectors, 20001 South Walnut Drive, Walnut, CA 91789.

Cost estimators. National Estimating Society, 101 S. Whiting Street, Alexandria, VA 22304; American Society of Professional Estimators, 6911 Richmond Highway, Alexandria, VA 22306.

Drywall workers and lathers. United Brotherhood of Carpenters (see also *Carpentry*); International Brotherhood of Painters and Allied Trades, 1750 New York Avenue NW, Washington, DC 20006; National Joint Painting, Decorating, and Drywall Apprenticeship and Training Committee, 1750 New York Avenue NW, Washington, DC 20006.

Electricians. Independent Electrical Contractors, Inc., 1101 Connecticut Avenue NW, Washington, DC 20036; International Brotherhood of Electrical Workers, 1125 15th Street NW, Washington, DC 20005; National Electrical Contractors Association, 7315 Wisconsin Avenue, Bethesda, MD 20814.

Glaziers. International Brotherhood of Painters and Allied Trades, 1750 New York Avenue NW, Washington, DC 20006; Membership Services, National Glass Association, 8200 Greensboro Drive, McLean, VA 22102.

Insulation workers. National Insulation and Abatement Contractors Association, 99 Canal Center Plaza, Alexandria, VA 22314.
Painters and paperhangers. International Brotherhood of Painters and Allied Trades, 1750 New York Avenue NW, Washington, DC 20006.
Plasterers. International Union of Bricklayers and Allied Craftsmen, 815 15th Street NW, Washington, DC 20005; Operative Plasterers' and Cement Masons' International Association of the United States and Canada, 1125 17th Street NW, Washington, DC 20036.
Plumbers and pipefitters. National Association of Plumbing-Heating-Cooling Contractors, P.O. Box 6806, Falls Church, VA 22046; National Fire Sprinkler Association, P.O. Box 1000, Patterson, NY 12563; Mechanical Contractors Association of America, 5410 Grosvenor Lane, Bethesda, MD 20814.
Roofers. National Roofing Contractors Association, 6250 River Road, Rosemont, IL 60018; United Union of Roofers, Waterproofers and Allied Workers, 1125 17th Street NW, Washington, DC 20036.
Sheet-metal workers. National Training Fund for the Sheet Metal and Air Conditioning Industry, Edward F. Carlough Plaza, 601 N. Fairfax Street, Alexandria, VA 22314.
Structural and reinforcing metal workers. International Association of Bridge, Structural and Ornamental Iron Workers, 1750 New York Avenue NW, Washington, DC 20006; National Erectors Association, 1501 Lee Highway, Arlington, VA 22209; National Association of Reinforcing Steel Contractors, 10382 Main Street, Fairfax, VA 22030.
Surveyors. American Congress on Surveying and Mapping, 210 Little Falls Street, Falls Church, VA 22046.
Tilesetters. International Union of Bricklayers and Allied Craftsmen, International Masonry Institute Apprenticeship and Training, 815 15th Street NW, Washington, DC 20005; Tile, Marble, Terrazzo Finishers, Shopworkers, and Granite Cutters International Union, 801 N. Pitt Street, Alexandria, VA 22314.
Excavation and loading machine operators (graders, dozers, scrapers, pavers, pipelayers, and so on). International Union of Operating Engineers, 1125 17th Street NW, Washington, DC

20036; Industrial Truck Association, 1750 K Street NW, Washington, DC 20006.

GOVERNMENT SERVICE

Village, city, township, county, state and federal government agencies offer secure job opportunities in virtually every category listed in this chapter. Clerical work (see Business Administration) offers the most opportunities, many in especially interesting and unusual areas. Court clerks, for example, must prepare court case dockets, do research and retrieve information for judges and contact witnesses, lawyers and litigants. There are thousands of other job opportunities in government for postal clerks, mail carriers, school crossing guards, emergency dispatchers, firefighters, highway maintenance workers, police officers, correction officers and other positions. Almost all government jobs require a high school diploma, six months experience and a passing score on the appropriate civil service examination. Salaries range from minimum wage to over $50,000 a year depending on the job and its responsibilities, the level of government and the region of the country. In general, civil service jobs do not pay as much as private industry, and promotions tend to be slower. But there are far more benefits (health insurance, guaranteed retirement pensions and so on), far greater job security, and pay increases are usually automatic and tied to the cost of living and length of time on the job. For more information, contact the Civil Service Commission of your state, county or city and the personnel department of the particular branch of government that interests you most. For federal jobs, contact the personnel department of the individual branch or the local Office of Personnel Management Job Information Center. The Office of Personnel Management (OPM) is what the federal government calls its civil service. OPM has branch offices and testing centers in most major cities. You can get the location and telephone number of the branch nearest you by calling (800)-555-1212. If you can't find one near you, write to Office of Personnel Management, P.O. Box 52, Washington, DC 20044 or telephone (202)-606-2700 and speak to an information specialist. For careers in the U.S. Postal Service, contact your local U.S. Post Office. For careers in protective services, contact your local government authorities and any organizations that follow:

The American Correctional Association, 8025 Laurel Lakes
  Court, Laurel, MD 20707
International Association of Fire Chiefs, 1329 18th Street NW,
  Washington, DC 20036
International Association of Fire Fighters, 1750 New York
  Avenue NW, Washington, DC 20006
National Fire Protection Association, Batterymarch Park, Quincy,
  MA 02269

Police officers, detectives, special agents.   Contact your local
state or city authorities. OPM handles all federal jobs in this field
except those at the FBI, which are handled by the FBI Applicant
Recruiting Office, 1900 Half Street SW, Washington, DC 20535.

HEALTH CARE

A high school diploma—and an interest in science and helping people—are all you need to take advantage of some exciting and almost
unlimited opportunities in the expanding field of health care. An associate degree from an accredited community college or technical institute opens up many more opportunities, of course, but you can get
started in the field with a diploma and move on at your own pace by
taking the necessary college courses part time. In addition to the specialized accreditation organizations that follow, make certain that any
health care program at a community or junior college or technical
institute is also *accredited* by one of these two organizations:

Committee of Allied Health Education and Accreditation
  (CAHEA) of the American Medical Association, 535 N.
  Dearborn Street, Chicago IL 60610
Accrediting Bureau of Health Education Schools (ABHES), Oak
  Manor Office, 29089 U.S. 20 West, Elkhart, IN 46514

Write to them both when exploring educational opportunities in the
health care field. Otherwise you may waste your time and money and
find yourself unqualified for state licensing—and a job.
  Here are the opportunities in this rapidly expanding field grouped
according to minimum educational requirements:

Health care careers requiring only a high school diploma
  Dispensing opticians.   Most dispensing opticians learn their trade
on the job. All that's required to enter the field is a pleasing per-

sonality to deal with patients and a high school diploma with a heavy concentration in math and science. High school physics, algebra, geometry and mechanical drawing are important, because training will include the study of optical mathematics, optical physics and use of precision measuring instruments for fitting patients with glasses. Apprenticeships lasting two to five years are required in 22 states to earn a license to practice. Formal training programs lasting from several weeks to two years are available at community colleges, technical institutes, trade schools and lens manufacturers. There are only 40 such programs in the United States and only 15 accredited by the Commission on Opticianry Accreditation, 10111 Martin Luther King Jr. Hwy., Suite 110, Bowie, MD 20715. Earnings for salaried dispensing opticians average about $25,000 a year and range from $15,000 to $30,000. Many experienced dispensing opticians go into business for themselves and earn far more—as much as $100,000 a year in some areas. For more information, write to the Opticians Association of America, 10341 Democracy Lane, P.O. Box 10110, Fairfax, VA 22030.

Emergency medical technicians (paramedics). The job requires a high school diploma plus a nine-month training program that includes the following three courses: a 110-hour Emergency Medical Technician's (EMT) course designed by the U.S. government and available in all 50 states and the District of Columbia at police, fire and health departments, hospitals and, as a nondegree course, at medical schools, colleges and universities; a two-day course on removing trapped victims; and a five-day course on driving emergency vehicles. For the EMT certificate, graduates of accredited EMT training programs must pass a written and practical exam administered by the National Registry of Emergency Medical Technicians. Earnings range from almost $17,000 to start to an average of about $32,000 a year for experienced paramedics. For further information write to your state's Emergency Medical Service Director at the state capital and to these two organizations: National Registry of Emergency Medical Technicians, P.O. Box 29223, Columbus, OH 43229 and National Association of Emergency Medical Technicians, 9140 Ward Parkway, Kansas City, MO 64114.

Licensed practical nurses. Rapid advances in medical technology may soon require a two-year associate degree from a community college. For now, however, most states only require a high school diploma and an LPN license available upon completion of a state-approved program given in high schools, community and junior colleges, hospitals and health agencies. Earnings range from $10,000 to $25,000 a year, depending on the area and the type of employer, and average about $21,500. The list of 1,250 approved training programs is available from the National League for Nursing, 350 Hudson Street, New York, NY 10014 and the National Association for Practical Nurse Education and Services, 1400 Spring Street, Silver Spring, MD 20910. Don't enroll in a program that's not on their lists. For more information on a career as an LPN, write to the National Federation of Licensed Practical Nurses, P.O. Box 1088, Durham, NC 27619.

Health care careers requiring an associate degree from community or junior college or technical institute

Electrocardiograph (EKG) technicians. The job requires a high school diploma with strong background in health, biology and typing and word processing. Training is on the job and usually lasts four to six weeks. Licensing by the National Board of Cardiovascular Testing (address follows) is voluntary but extremely valuable in getting better jobs in this field. Salaries range from about $13,000 a year as a hospital trainee to $25,000 for experienced technicians. Lists of training programs are available from the National Society for Cardiovascular Technology/National Society of Pulmonary Technology, 1133 15th Street NW, Suite 1000, Washington, DC 20005. For information on credentials, write to the Cardiovascular Credentialing International and National Board of Cardiovascular Testing, P.O. Box 611, Wright Brothers Station, Dayton, OH 45419-0611.

Dental hygienists. This is an exciting career yielding annual earnings ranging between $12,500 and $25,000, usually *part time* at an average pay of $14 to $15 an hour in association with a private dental practice or in a school system, hospital or public health agency. Hygienists must be licensed by the state. That requires a two-year associate degree from one of the nearly 200 schools of dental hygiene accredited by the Commission on Dental Accreditation of the American Dental Association (ADA) *and* passing a written and clinical examination administered by the ADA Joint

Commission on National Dental Examinations. For a list of accredited programs write to the Commission on Dental Accreditation, American Dental Association, 211 E. Chicago Avenue, Suite 1814, Chicago, IL 60611. For information on careers in dental hygiene, write the Division of Professional Development, American Dental Hygienists' Association, 444 N. Michigan Ave., Suite 3400, Chicago, IL 60611.

Medical laboratory technicians. These technicians perform a wide range of routine tests and laboratory procedures in hospitals, clinics, and medical and research laboratories. Training can be on the job, but most lab technicians have at least a two-year associate degree from a community college. Earnings range from minimum wage to $30,000 a year depending on the area of the country and the type of institution. Write to the Accrediting Bureau of Health Education Schools, 29089 U.S. 20 West, Elkhart, IN 46514 for a list of accredited training programs. No one will hire a lab technician who does not graduate from an *accredited* program. Certification is voluntary, but it's a valuable credential that is often required as an indication of professional competence. Write to the National Certification Agency for Medical Laboratory Personnel, 1101 Connecticut Avenue NW, Washington, DC 20036.

Medical record technicians. A key figure in hospital care, the medical record technician is in charge of patient medical histories and charts essential for proper treatment and care. Training is available in about 100 two-year associate degree programs accredited by CAHEA. Training includes courses in biological sciences, medical terminology, medical record science, business management, legal aspects of medical and hospital practices and computer data processing. After graduation, medical record technicians obtain professional credentials by passing a written exam of the American Medical Record Association at the same address as the accreditation committee. Earnings range from more than $13,000 to more than $25,000 a year. Contact the American Medical Record Association, 875 N. Michigan Avenue, John Hancock Center, Chicago, IL 60611.

Radiologic (X-ray) technicians. Technicians in physicians' offices who only take routine X rays are usually trained on the job and need only a high school diploma. The more complex work in hospitals and medical centers requires one to two years of formal training in radiography, radiation therapy technology and diagnostic medical sonography (ultrasound). There are more than 750 programs—mostly two-year associate degree programs at community colleges and technical institutes—accredited by CAHEA. New technology such as magnetic resonance imaging is making this one of the fastest growing sectors of health care with starting salaries averaging more than $17,000 a year and earnings of experienced radiologic technologists *averaging* about $25,000. The top of the range reaches as high as $40,000. Contact the following organizations: American Society of Radiologic Technologists, 15000 Central Avenue SE, Albuquerque, NM 87123; Society of Diagnostic Medical Sonographers, 12225 Greenville Avenue, Dallas, TX 75231; American Registry of Radiologic Technologists, 1255 Northland Drive, Mendota, MN 55120; and American Registry of Diagnostic Medical Sonographers, 32 Hollister Street, Cincinnati, OH 45219.

Registered nurses. With more patient care responsibilities being handed over to registered nurses, there is growing pressure to make all R.N.s obtain a four-year bachelor's degree. For now, however, there are two other training programs available—a two-year associate degree from community and junior colleges and a three-year diploma program given in hospitals. Both of them, along with four-year R.N. programs at colleges and universities, qualify graduates for entry-level positions as hospital staff nurses. Earnings range from $15,000 to $40,000 and are likely to climb as the nursing shortage grows. Nurses also earn extra pay for working evening and night shifts. Don't confuse a *registered nurse* with a practical nurse (LPN) or any other kind of nurse. To become a registered nurse requires attending an accredited program leading to a degree as an R.N. from one of the more than 1,400 accredited programs and a *license,* which is only available after passing a national examination administered by each state. For more information, write to American Nurses' Association, 2420 Pershing Road, Kansas City, MO 64108; American Hospital Association, Division of Nursing, 840 North Lake Shore Drive, Chicago, IL 60611; American Health Care Association, 1201 L Street NW, Washington, DC 20005.

Surgical technicians. Although there are about 200 training programs, only about 100 are approved by CAHEA. A high school diploma is required for admission to these programs, which last at least 9 to 10 months when taken on the job in hospitals but extend to two years at community and junior colleges awarding associate degrees. The shorter, in-hospital programs are generally limited to licensed practical or registered nurses with experience in patient care. The work involves preparing patients for surgery, setting up the operating room and passing instruments and other materials to surgeons and surgeons' assistants during an operation. Starting salaries average about $15,000 a year and, depending on education, experienced technologists can earn about $20,000 a year. Write to the Association of Surgical Technologists, 8307 Shaffer Parkway, Littleton, CO 80127.

HOSPITALITY

Food and beverage preparation

Chefs, cooks and other kitchen workers need no formal education to start. They can learn all their skills on the job. But that's the hard way. An easier and better way is to get a high school diploma, a strong background in business mathematics and business administration courses and formal training in either an apprenticeship program or a two-year or four-year college. Apprenticeship programs last up to three years and are offered by professional culinary institutes, industry trade associations and trade unions. Two-year community colleges offer associate degrees and a few four-year colleges and universities offer a bachelor degree. Some high schools offer courses in food preparation, but these seldom have any value for obtaining any but the least-skilled jobs in the lowest-paying sectors of the industry, such as fast-food restaurants. Formal training at an accredited culinary institute or other advanced educational institution is the surest way to a good job. For a directory of two-year and four-year colleges with courses in the food service field, write to the Educational Foundation of the National Restaurant Association, 250 South Wacker Drive, Suite 1400, Chicago, IL 60606. Also write for a directory of colleges and schools from the Council on Hotel, Restaurant and Institutional Education, 1200 17th Street, NW, Washington, DC 20036-3097. There's some duplication in the two catalogs, but it's worth having them both. Also write to the National Association of Trade and Technical Schools, P.O. Box 10429, Rockville, MD 20850, for a directory of accredited private trade schools and culinary institutes that may not be listed in the other catalogs. And finally, write to the

American Culinary Federation, P.O. Box 3466, St. Augustine, FL 32084, which offers apprenticeship programs and certifies chefs at the levels of cook, chef, pastry chef, executive chef and master chef. Earnings in the food preparation field vary widely, from minimum wage for inexperienced beginners to $100,000 a year for world-renowned master chefs at elegant French restaurants in cities such as New York or San Francisco. On average, however, food preparation personnel earn between $9,000 and $20,000 a year depending on years of experience, position in the kitchen hierarchy and type of restaurant. Fast-food restaurants pay the least—usually minimum wage, regardless of experience. Elegant "white-tablecloth" restaurants usually pay the most but demand the most experience. In many areas, especially in big cities, hotel and restaurant workers must join unions.

Food and beverage service workers
This category includes dining room attendants (busboys and busgirls), bartender assistants, serving persons, hosts and hostesses and bartenders. Most bartenders go to private trade schools for a standard two-week course (contact National Association of Trade and Technical Schools, P.O. Box 10429, Rockville, MD 20850 for a list of accredited schools), but all other food and beverage service work is learned on the job. Most employers prefer applicants with high school diplomas, a solid grounding in mathematics (for accurate handling of meal charges) and pleasing personalities. Pay ranges from minimum wage to $20,000 a year for an experienced host or hostess who has been on the job for many years at an elegant "white tablecloth" restaurant in a major city. Average earnings, however, are about $12,000 a year; but tips, which run between 15% and 20% of guest checks for waiters and waitresses, can double the totals. Bartenders earn similar salaries and can also double their incomes with tips. More information on hospitality careers is available from the Council on Hotel, Restaurant, and Institutional Education, 1200 17th Street, NW, Washington, DC 20036-3097; the Educational Foundation of the National Restaurant Association, 250 South Wacker Drive, Chicago, IL 60606; and the National Association of Trade and Technical Schools, P.O. Box 10429, Rockville, MD 20850.

Other career opportunities in hospitality:
- Amusement and recreation park attendants, fee collectors, carnival and amusement park ride and concession stand operators, facility

preparers at indoor game parlors (billiards, pinball machines, video machines and so on), servers at sports clubs and spas.
- Hotel baggage porters and bellhops.
- Business administration: hotels, amusement and theme parks, restaurants, stadiums and sports arenas. Clerical functions (office clerks, secretaries, reservations clerks, desk clerks and cashiers) are as essential to the hospitality industry as they are to every other industry. Basic training for these jobs, along with cash and materials management, desk clerks, operators, cashiers and receptionists is discussed in the section on Business Administration. Additional training to adapt business administration skills to the hospitality industry should take place on-the-job, although some might want to consider courses in hotel and restaurant administration at a community or technical college. Some institutions, such as Hocking Technical College in Ohio, operate their own motel, restaurant, travel agency and support systems as part of their Hospitality Program.
- Housekeeping. See "Janitors and cleaners" under Service Occupations.
- Sports and activities supervision. See Sports and Recreation.
- Maintenance. See "Grounds maintenance" under Agriculture or "Janitors and cleaners" under Service Occupations.
- Theater ushers, lobby attendants, ticket takers, cashiers.

MARKETING AND SALES

Retailing
Retailing offers many job opportunities as cashiers, wrappers, floor and counter sales clerks and stock clerks in all types of consumer outlets, specialty stores, supermarkets, department stores, theaters, laundries, dry cleaners, video rental stores and car rental agencies to name a few. All training is on-the-job and applicants don't need high school diplomas, although employers prefer a strong background in mathematics for handling cash accurately and a pleasing personality for dealing diplomatically with customers. To advance into management ranks or to go into business for yourself, however, a high school diploma and at least a community college associate degree in business administration are essential. Some high schools call their vocational programs for retailing "Distributive Education." Don't let the fancy name confuse you. As for earnings, small stores—those with less than about $400,000 in annual sales—are not even required to

pay minimum wage. Some stores pay salespeople as much as $20,000
a year. Others (furniture stores, for example) pay salary plus commission, which can lift top earnings still higher. The *average* salesperson in all areas of retailing only earns about $12,000 a year; but
the average salary in specific areas can vary widely, depending on
the products sold. Car and boat salespeople average more than $25,000
a year, and the best salespeople in such "big ticket" trades earn
upwards of $50,000 a year. Appliance and furniture salespeople av-
erage almost $20,000 a year, while door-to-door salespeople average
about $25,000. Apparel salespeople earn an average of about $12,000
a year.

Real estate agents

Although real estate agents must be licensed in every state, most
states do not require a college degree. All that's necessary is to pass
a 90-hour course that is offered by many large real estate firms and
by more than 1,000 universities, colleges, and junior and community
colleges. At some colleges, students can earn an associate degree or
bachelor degree in real estate. Average earnings were more than
$40,000 a year during the real estate boom of the late 1980s, but
dropped dramatically in 1990 and 1991 along with job opportunities.
For career information and a list of colleges offering courses in real
estate, contact the National Association of Realtors, 430 North Michigan Avenue, Chicago, IL 60611.

Wholesale sales

Wholesalers, who buy goods from manufacturers and resell them to
retailers, have armies of salespeople who sell in two ways: "Inside"
salespeople solicit sales by telephone, while "outside" salespeople
sell by personal solicitation with visits to retail store owners and managers. The variety of products sold by wholesalers is as wide as the
variety of products in any department or discount store. Wholesale
trade salespeople are usually hired directly out of high school and
trained on-the-job—first as stock clerks to become familiar with the
merchandise the wholesaler may carry and the complex pricing of
such goods. Initial training generally leads to "inside" sales jobs,
first as an order taker on incoming reorders from steady customers,
then eventually as a troubleshooter soliciting telephone orders from
customers who have not reordered. After two years on the inside, top
salespeople acquire outside sales routes. Community college courses

in wholesale distribution, marketing and business administration can speed advancement into management. Wholesale trade salespeople earn as little as $6,000 a year as trainees but quickly rise into the $20,000 to $40,000 range when they become outside salespeople. Top salespeople earn upwards of $50,000 a year. Other career opportunities in wholesaling include the range of business administration functions (see Business Administration) and inventory controls and handling stock as it moves on and off company shelves. Stock work is usually a minimum wage job, but salaries improve with increased responsibilities.

MECHANICAL TRADES

The mechanical trades—mechanics, installers and repairers—offer some of the widest opportunities for personal and financial success of any professional area. Mechanics keep America's machinery running. They are the men and women who make it safe for us to fly in airplanes and ride in cars, trucks, transit systems and building elevators; they make it safe to use home appliances and keep our heating and cooling equipment operating; they keep us in touch with the world by maintaining and repairing communications equipment such as telephones, radios, televisions and computers. American industry could not produce the goods and services we all need without mechanics to keep production machinery humming. Indeed, without mechanics, our nation would be unable to function.

Here are just a few of the opportunities in this enormously important field of installation, maintenance and repair: aircraft and aircraft engines; diesel engines; cars and trucks; car bodies; office equipment and cash registers; computers; commercial and industrial electronic equipment (everything from radar and missile installations to medical diagnostic equipment); telephones and communications equipment; television and stereos; elevators; farm equipment; heating; air-conditioning; refrigeration equipment; home appliances and power tools; industrial machinery; heavy equipment; vending machines; musical instruments; boats and motorcycles and small engines. Any piece of equipment you can think of needs an expert who knows how it works to keep it running smoothly and fix it when it breaks down. That person is a mechanic.

Years ago, it used to be easy for anyone with "good hands" to go into the mechanical trades, even without a high school diploma. But like the field of business administration, the mechanical trades have become an area of constant change due to rapid technological advances. As in business administration, automation and other devices are eliminating jobs. They're not eliminating careers—just jobs. The auto repair business, for example, still offers wonderful career opportunities, but the job of hand-tuning engines on most cars has disappeared. The same is true in all areas of the mechanical trades, and that's why today's mechanics must be so well-educated.

A high school diploma is virtually a must in every area of mechanical trades along with a solid understanding of mathematics and basic scientific principles (especially physics), and the ability to read and understand complex materials relating to the functioning and repairing of complex machinery and equipment.

In addition to academic requirements, entry into most mechanical trades requires two to four years of solid vocational education either in high school, an accredited trade school, community college or a formal company training program. And finally, at least two to four years on-the-job are needed to reach the status of master craftsperson. The rewards for this investment in time and study can be great. There are mechanics in almost every specialty previously mentioned earning as much as $50,000 a year. Computer service technicians, for example, usually start at about $17,500 a year, average more than $25,000 within five years and can earn $40,000 to $50,000 when they reach the top of their trade. Diesel engine mechanics in the transportation industry *average* $30,000 a year or more. So, the demand for mechanics is great, and so are the rewards.

As in every other professional area, it's important to get the proper training. What follows are organizations which will send you career information, certification requirements (if any) and lists of accredited schools and colleges for each mechanical trade:

Aircraft

Aviation Maintenance Foundation, P.O. Box 2826, Redmond, WA 98073
(career information)
Professional Aviation Maintenance Association, 500 Northwest Plaza,
St. Ann, MO 63074 (career information)

Automotive

Automotive Service Association, Inc., P.O. Box 929, Bedford, TX 76021-
0929 (career information)

Automotive Service Industry Association, 444 North Michigan Avenue, Chicago, IL 60611 (career information)

Motor and Equipment Manufacturers Association, Technical Training Council, 300 Sylvan Avenue, Englewood Cliffs, NJ 07632 (training information)

National Automotive Technical Education Foundation, 13505 Dulles Technology Drive, Herndon, VA 22071-3415 (list of certified automotive training programs)

Commercial and industrial electronic equipment
Electronic Technicians Association, 604 North Jackson, Greencastle, IN 46135 (career, certification and placement information)

International Society of Certified Electronics Technicians, 2708 West Berry Street, Fort Worth, TX 76109 (career and certification information)

Communications equipment
line installers and splicers
Communications Workers of America, 1925 K Street NW, Washington, DC 20006 (employment opportunities)

International Brotherhood of Electrical Workers, 1125 15th Street NW, Washington, DC 20005 (career information)

United States Telephone Association, 900 19th Street NW, Washington, DC 20006 (career information)

Your local telephone or long distance company (career opportunities)

Diesel mechanics
ASE, 13505 Dulles Technology Drive, Herndon, VA 22071-3415 (training information)

American Trucking Association, 2200 Mill Road, Alexander, VA 22314 (career information)

Automotive Service Industry Association, 444 North Michigan Avenue, Chicago, IL 60611 (career information)

International Association of Machinists and Aerospace Workers, Apprenticeship Department, 1300 Connecticut Avenue NW, Washington, DC 20036 (career and training information)

Motor and Equipment Manufacturers Association, Technical Training Council, 300 Sylvan Avenue, Englewood Cliffs, NJ 07632 (training information)

National Institute for Automotive Service Excellence, 1920 Association Drive, Reston, VA 22091 (certification information)

Electronic and home entertainment equipment

Electronic Industries Association, 2001 I Street NW, Washington, DC 20006 (career information)

National Electronic Sales and Service Dealers Association and the International Society of Certified Electronics Technicians, 2708 West Berry Street, Fort Worth, TX 76109 (career and certification information)

Electronics Technicians Association, 604 North Jackson, Greencastle, IN 46135 (career information)

Farm equipment

North American Equipment Dealers Association, 10877 Watson Road, Street Louis, MO 63127 (career information)

Motor and Equipment Manufacturers Association, Technical Training Council, 300 Sylvan Avenue, Englewood, NJ 07632 (training information)

Heating, air-conditioning and refrigeration

Associated Builders & Contractors, 729 15th Street NW, Washington DC 20005 (career information)

National Association of Plumbing, Heating, and Cooling Contractors, P.O. Box 6808, Falls Church, VA 22046 (career information)

Refrigeration Service Engineers Society, 1666 Rand Road, Des Plaines, IL 60016 (career information)

Heavy equipment (bulldozers, and so on)

Motor and Equipment Manufacturers Association, Technical Training Council, 300 Sylvan Avenue, Englewood Cliffs, NJ 07632 (career information)

Industrial machinery

International Union of Electronic, Electrical, Salaried, Machine and Furniture Workers, 1126 16th Street NW, Washington, DC 20036 (career opportunities and apprenticeship programs)

Millwrights

(Note: Millwrights install and dismantle the machinery and heavy equipment used in virtually every factory in America. They're the mechanics who unpack, inspect and set into place all new production machinery with cranes or whatever other equipment is needed. Earnings can reach above $40,000 a year, depending on the area of the country.)

Associated General Contractors of America, 1957 E Street NW, Washington, DC 20006 (career information)

Small engines (motorcycles, boats, and so on)
Motor and Equipment Manufacturers Association, 300 Sylvan Avenue, Englewood Cliffs, NJ 07632 (career information)

Musical instruments (repair and tuning)
National Association of Professional Band Instrument Repair Technicians, P.O. Box 51, Normal, IL 61761 (career information)
Piano Technicians Guild, 9140 Ward Parkway, Kansas City, MO 64114 (career information and list of accredited schools offering courses)

Vending machines
National Automatic Merchandising Association, 20 N. Wacker Drive, Chicago, IL 60606 (list of accredited schools)

Other career opportunities (on-the-job or private trade school training only)
Bicycle repairs, medical equipment repairs, instrument and tool repairs, rail car repairs, rigging, tire repairs, watch repairs.

Additional information
National Association of Trade and Technical Schools, P.O. Box 10429, Rockville, MD 20850 (list of accredited private trade schools)
Your state labor department (in the state capital) for lists of apprenticeship programs in various trades
Your state employment service (job opportunities)

PERFORMING ARTS

Unlike other professions, there is no sure way to success in the performing arts. Many talented actors, singers and dancers have spent their lifetime waiting tables in restaurants only steps away from Broadway theaters—waiting for the "big break" that never came. And many performers with questionable talents have made millions because they did get a "big break," or perhaps they had the right "connections." In either case, there are factors beyond one's control that can affect careers in the performing arts far more than in many other professions where study and hard work are usually the surest means of success.

Unlike many other professions, too, the performing arts offer opportunities for men and women with widely varying levels of formal education. Many have university degrees; others dropped out of high school and never spent another minute studying their crafts. Obviously, careers in classical music, ballet or theater require years of formal study. That's not necessarily the case for careers in popular music, dance or theater. What most successful artists have in common, however, is talent, and most have spent years practicing what they do—whether it's acting, singing, dancing, playing a musical instrument or announcing on radio and television. Those who stayed in school have worked on school and college productions of all kinds or in local theater groups and informal musical groups.

Formal training can be a big help, because it often puts students in touch with professionals and job opportunities. Formal study in most of the performing arts is available at all levels: high schools, community colleges, four-year colleges and universities and private trade schools. For high school students, the finest education in the performing arts is at so-called "magnet" schools such as LaGuardia High School (once known as the High School of Performing Arts in New York City, the school portrayed in the TV show "Fame"). There are similar magnet schools in other major cities, all part of the public school system of their states. But admission is competitive by audition and restricted to the most-talented applicants.

In some states such as North Carolina, magnet schools have boarding facilities for applicants who live too far away to commute. Many community colleges and four-year universities have outstanding departments in one or more of the performing arts. Check with the state superintendent of schools to see if there are any magnet high schools for the performing arts in your state. Use the various guides to two-year and four-year colleges to identify those with outstanding music, theater or dance departments. Peterson's directory of two-year colleges even has a form you can send in with your special areas of interest, and the publisher's computer will pick all the appropriate schools for you to contact. Barron's Educational Series (250 Wireless Blvd., Hauppauge, NY 11788) has helpful guides for four-year colleges, universities and graduate schools, The National Association of Trade and Technical Schools (see Appendix A) lists accredited trade schools for acting.

The performing arts also includes behind-the-scenes opportunities discussed elsewhere. These include broadcast technicians (see Technical Trades), administrative and clerical work (see Business Administration), camera crews (see Arts and Crafts, Photography and Camera Work), instrument tuning and maintenance (see Mechanical Trades), set design (see Arts and Crafts, Design) and carpentry and electrical work (see Construction Trades).

PRODUCTION TRADES

Production workers make every product produced by American industry—apparel, fabrics and textiles, toys, furniture, home furnishings, shoes and leather goods, books and publications, tools and machinery, eyeglass rims, dental bridges, jewelry, cars, ladders and every other product you can think of. It's an endless list. Everything you see around you has to be made by hand or machine. The products that are mass-produced by machine are made by production workers who earn between $10,000 and $50,000 a year depending on the area of the country, the specific industry and the skills and training involved. Tool and die makers, who need four to five years of apprenticeship training, are in great demand. They earn about $15,000 to start and average nearly $30,000 after several years. The top 10% of their craft earn more than $50,000 a year. Most production workers earn between $12,000 and $15,000 to start. In 1988, earnings for production work averaged $22,000 a year for all industries and ranged from $20,000 to $30,000 a year for workers with five to 10 years experience. Skilled workers able to deal effectively with people can work their way up to supervisory positions as inspectors, graders, testers and, of course, production line and plant floor supervisors. Those jobs usually pay between $25,000 and $50,000 a year. Almost all training for production work is on-the-job, either in a formal apprenticeship program or as an assistant to a skilled worker who serves as a mentor. Not all industries require workers to have high school diplomas, but in today's world of advanced technology, most manufacturers prefer applicants with high school diplomas and strong backgrounds in math, science (especially physics) and English (for reading complex instructions). Many high schools, vocational schools, community colleges, technical institutes and private trade schools offer formal training in specific production areas. Here is a sampling of the types of production trades and the organizations to contact for more information about career opportunities and training programs.

Apparel workers
American Apparel Manufacturers Association, 2500 Wilson Blvd., Arlington, VA 22201
Check college directories for specialized textile colleges.

Bakers, butchers, meat-poultry-fish cutters, cooking machine operators, dairy processors
United Food & Commercial Workers International Union, 1775 K Street NW, Washington, DC 20006

Bindery workers (production of books, magazines, catalogs, folders, directories)
Education Council of the Graphic Arts Industry, 4615 Forbes Avenue, Pittsburgh, PA 15213
Graphic Communications International Union, 1900 L Street NW, Washington, DC 20036
Binding Industries of America, 70 East Lake Street, Chicago, IL 60601

Compositors and typesetters, lithographers and photoengravers, printing press operator, screen printing setters
Education Council of the Graphic Arts Industry, 4615 Forbes Avenue, Pittsburgh, PA 15213
National Composition Association of the Printing Industries of America, 1730 N. Lynn Street, Arlington, VA 22209
Graphic Communications International Union, 1900 L Street NW, Washington, DC 20036

Dental laboratory technicians (production and repair of dental fittings and appliances)
American Dental Association Commission on Dental Accreditation, Division of Educational Measurement, 211 E. Chicago Avenue, Chicago, IL 60611
National Association of Dental Laboratories, 3801 Mt. Vernon Avenue, Alexandria, VA 22305

**Electric power generating plant operators,
power distributors and dispatchers**
Edison Electric Institute, 1111 19th Street NW, Washington, DC 20005
International Brotherhood of Electrical Workers, 1125 15th Street NW,
 Washington, DC 20005
Utility Workers Union of America, 815 16th Street NW, Washington,
 DC 20006

Jewelers
Jewelers of America, Time-Life Bldg, 1271 Avenue of the Americas,
 New York, NY 10020

**Machinists and metalworkers, numerical-control machine
tool operators, plastics fabrication machine operators, tool
and die makers, metal fabricators, sheet-metal workers,
metal pourers and casters, extruding and forming machine
operators**
The National Machine Tool Builders Association, 7901 Westport Drive,
 McLean, VA 22102
The National Tooling & Machining Association, 9300 Livingston Road,
 Fort Washington, MD 20744
National Screw Machine Products Association, 6700 W. Snowville Road,
 Brecksville, OH 44141
The Tooling and Manufacturing Association, 1177 South Dee Road, Park
 Ridge, IL 60068

**Ophthalmic laboratory technicians (production of optical
goods and eyeglasses)**
Commission on Opticianry Accreditation, 10111 Martin Luther King Jr.
 Highway, Bowie, MD 20715

Painting and coating machine operators
Automotive Service Industry Association, 444 North Michigan Avenue,
 Chicago, IL 60611
Automotive Service Association, P.O. Box 929, Bedford, TX 76021
National Institute for Automotive Service Excellence, 13505 Dulles
 Technology Drive, Herndon, VA 22071-3415

Photographic process workers
Photo Marketing Association International, 3000 Picture Place, Jackson,
 MI 49201

Shoe and leather workers
Prescription Footwear Association, 9861 Broken Land Parkway, Columbia, MD 21046

Stationary (operating) engineers (operation and maintenance repair of power generating equipment)
International Union of Operating Engineers, 1125 17th Street NW, Washington, DC 20036
National Association of Power Engineers, 2350 East Devon Street, Des Plaines, IL 60018

Textile machinery operators
American Textile Manufacturers Institute, 1801 K Street NW, Washington, DC 20006
American Fiber Manufacturers Association, 1150 17th Street NW, Washington, DC 20036

Water and waste water treatment plant operators
National Environmental Training Association, 8687 Via de Ventura, Scottsdale, AZ 85258
Water Pollution Control Federation, 601 Wythe Street, Alexandria, VA 22314.

Welders, solderers, brazers, cutters and welding machine operators
American Welding Society, 550 NW LeJeune Road, Miami, FL 33126
National Association of Trade and Technical Schools, P.O. Box 10429, Rockville, MD 10850

Woodworking
American Furniture Manufacturers Association, Manufacturing Services Division, P.O. Box HP-7, High Point, NC 27261
Institute for Woodworking Education, 1012 Tenth Street, Manhattan Beach, CA 90266.
International Woodworkers of America, U.S. Research and Education Department, 25 Cornell Avenue, Gladstone, OR 97027

Other career opportunities in production trades
(on-the-job and trade school training only)
Boiler operators; cannery workers; chemical equipment controllers and
operators; chemical plant and system operators; coil winders and ta-
pers; crushing and mixing machine operators; cutting and slicing machine operators; electrical and electronic assemblers; electronic sem-
iconductor processors; furnace, kiln and kettle operators; gas and
petroleum plant and systems operations; hand grinders and polishers;
laundry and dry-cleaning machine operators; machine assemblers;
machine feeders and offbearers; miners; packagers; quarry workers;
roustabouts (oil field workers); tunneling machine operators; packaging and filling machine operators; separating and still machine operators; shipfitters and tirebuilding machine operators.

SERVICE OCCUPATIONS

Barbers
No high school diploma is required, but all states require barbers to
be licensed. That means attending a state-approved barber school (9
to 12 months), then taking an examination for an apprentice license,
working as an apprentice for one to two years and, finally, taking
another examination for a license as a registered barber. Barbers seldom earn salaries. Instead, they earn 60% to 70% of the money they
take in—and they get to keep all tips. Earnings, which vary widely
from area to area, range from about $6,500 a year for beginners to
$25,000 for experienced hairstylists—plus tips. Many barbers own
their shops and earn more. A list of accredited barber schools is
available from the National Association of Barber Schools, 304 South
11th Street, Lincoln, NE 68502.

Childcare workers
Although no experience or formal training is required, most day care
centers and other employers expect workers to have at least a high
school education and to have studied some psychology, sociology,
home economics, nutrition, art, music, drama and physical education. Moreover, a growing number of employers now require formal
training and certification in childcare at the community college level.
Many high schools and community colleges offer a training program
leading to a Child Development Associate (CDA) certificate. The
program is open to anyone at least 18 years old with some childcare

experience or related classroom training. For details, write to CDA National Credentialing Program, 1718 Connecticut Avenue NW, Washington, DC 20009. Earnings in childcare are low, starting at minimum wage for beginners and seldom exceeding $15,000 a year.

Cosmetologists (beauticians and hairstylists)

State requirements vary, but all states require licensing, and that means being at least 16 years old, passing a physical examination and graduating from a state-licensed school of cosmetology. Some states require a high school diploma; others only require an eighth grade education. Unlike barbering, cosmetology instruction is offered in both public and private schools. Public high schools and vocational schools usually offer free training combined with useful academic education. Private trade schools, which charge fees, only teach the trade. Students in both public and private cosmetology schools must buy their own tools. Day courses usually take six months to a year to complete, while evening courses take longer. After graduation, cosmetologists must take a state licensing examination, part written and part practical demonstration. Earnings vary widely from area to area but usually range from $10,000 to $15,000 to start and between $15,000 and $25,000 for experienced professionals. Tips are an important factor, and many cosmetologists in wealthy communities earn between $30,000 and $50,000 a year. Gifted cosmetologists can earn even more working with a private clientele or in the performing arts—television, movies and theater—preparing actors and actresses for performances. For additional information contact the National Accrediting Commission of Cosmetology Arts and Sciences, 1333 H Street NW, Washington, DC 20005; National Association of Accredited Cosmetology Schools, 5201 Leesburg Pike, Falls Church, VA 22041; National Cosmetology Association, 3510 Olive Street, St. Louis, MO 63103; and Hair International, 1318 Starbrook Drive, Charlotte, NC 28210.

Homemaker and home health aides

Although a high school diploma is desirable, most agencies only require an ability to read, write and complete a one- to two-week training program as a homemaker/home health aide, which the agencies usually pay for. Some agencies and states require a nursing aide certificate. Earnings range from $3.50 to $6.00 an hour for a 20 to 36 hour work week. The National Association for Homecare (519 C Street NE, Stanton Park, Washington, DC 20002) has more details on training and career opportunities.

Building custodians (janitors) and cleaners
Most training is on-the-job, although workers must know simple arithmetic, how to read and write and how to make simple repairs. Shop courses at school can be helpful. No other formal education is required. Earnings range from minimum wage to nearly $25,000 a year depending on the area of the country, hours worked and type of employer. About one-third of the more than 2.5 million janitors and cleaners work part time, that is, less than 35 hours a week. The largest employers are schools (including colleges and universities) and private maintenance firms, which clean buildings under contract. These two sectors employ about 20% each of the custodial work force. Hospitals and hotels each employ 10%, and the rest of the custodial force works in restaurants, apartment buildings, office buildings, manufacturing plants, government buildings and churches and other religious buildings. The field offers outstanding opportunities for experienced custodians willing to study small business management to establish private-home and apartment cleaning services. More information is available from the Building Service Contractors Association, 10201 Lee Highway, Fairfax, VA 22030.

Pest control
This is usually a minimum wage job, although opportunities for self-employment after learning the trade can raise the annual income to between $30,000 and $50,000.

Private household workers
Usually no training or formal education is required, although most employers insist on an ability to clean well and/or cook and/or take care of children—skills generally learned while helping with housework at home. Courses in home economics, cooking, childcare, child development, first aid and nursing can lead to broader opportunities and better-paying jobs. Two-thirds of the one million private household workers work part time. Earnings range from minimum wage to $10 an hour, depending on the area of the country. Live-in workers earn more, between $400 and $1,000 a week, but such jobs require

special training at schools for butlers, chauffeurs, nannies, governesses and cooks.

SPORTS AND RECREATION

Recreation workers are needed on a full-time or part-time basis at various establishments—commercial recreation areas, hotels, resorts, amusement parks, sports and entertainment centers, wilderness and survival excursion companies, tourist centers, vacation excursion firms, camps, health spas, athletic clubs, apartment and condominium complexes, ocean liners, civic and religious organizations, social service organizations (day care and senior citizens centers), residential care facilities and institutions, industrial plants and city, state and federal parks. To work at most schools and colleges, recreation workers and coaches must have a bachelor's degree in physical education from a four-year college and a teaching certificate. For other areas mentioned, only a high school diploma may be required along with experience in one or more recreational areas (art, music, drama and so on) or sports. Some jobs, such as lifeguards, require special certification. For career-track jobs, most employers now require an associate degree in park and recreation programs (available at about 200 community and junior colleges). Earnings range from $12,000 to $30,000 a year. Write to the National Recreation and Park Association, 3101 Park Center Drive, Alexandria, VA 22302, for career information, a list of approved academic programs and a twice-monthly bulletin of job opportunities. Additional information is available from the American Association for Leisure and Recreation, 1900 Association Drive, Reston, VA 22091; the National Employee Services and Recreation Association, 2400 South Downing Street, Westchester, IL 60153; and the American Camping Association, Bradford Woods, 5000 State Road, 67 N, Martinsville, IN 46151. For careers with the YMCA, write the YMCA National Office, 101 North Wacker Drive, Chicago, IL 60606.

TECHNICAL TRADES

Air traffic controllers
Formal training is an intensive 11 to 13 weeks at the Federal Aviation Administration (FAA) Academy in Oklahoma City followed by several years of combined on-the-job and classroom training to learn the

U.S. airway system. Applicants must be high school graduates under 31 years old and pass federal civil service physical and psychological examinations. In general, they must also have three years work experience, a solid knowledge of aviation and be highly skilled in mathematics, science and English and have high aptitudes in abstract reasoning and three-dimensional visualization. Starting salaries are just under $20,000 a year. Experienced controllers average about $40,000 a year. Air traffic controllers are federal government employees. For more information, contact the U.S. Office of Personnel Management Job Information Center nearest you—call "800" information, (800) 555-1212, for the telephone number—and ask for a copy of the Air Traffic Controller Announcement.

Broadcast technicians
An associate degree from a technical institute or community college is required for operating and maintaining the complex electronic equipment, which records and transmits radio and television programs. Also required is a radio-telephone operator license issued by the Federal Communications Commission after successful completion of a series of written exams. Those entering the field must have strong backgrounds in high school algebra, trigonometry, physics, electronics and other sciences. Starting jobs at small stations pay about $15,000. As a profession, technicians average between $20,000 and $25,000 but can earn $50,000 or more at network-owned radio and television stations. Supervisory jobs can pay close to $100,000 at such stations. For information on licensing procedures, write the Federal Communications Commission, 1919 M Street NW, Washington, DC 20554. For career information, write to the National Association of Broadcasters Employment Clearinghouse, 1771 N Street NW, Washington, DC 20036 and to the National Cable Television Association, 1724 Massachusetts Avenue NW, Washington, DC 20036. For a list of accredited schools, write to the Broadcast Education Association, National Association of Broadcasters, 1771 N Street NW, Washington, DC 20036. For information on certification, write to the Society of Broadcast Engineers, 7002 Graham Road, Indianapolis, IN 46220.

Computer programmers
Taught at public and private vocational schools, community colleges and four-year colleges, computer programming pays between $15,000

and $50,000 a year depending on experience with average income just under $30,000. Most of the 500,000 employees in this fast-growing area work for firms that write and sell computer software, manufacturing firms, government agencies, banks, insurance companies, and colleges and universities. Write to the Institute for the Certification of Computer Professionals, 2200 East Devon Avenue, Des Plaines, IL 60018.

Drafters

Drafting—the drawing of exact design dimensions and specifications of every product and part that is manufactured and every structure that is built—is a profession requiring a two-year associate degree from a technical institute, community college or trade school. Training includes courses in mathematics, physics, mechanical drawing and, of course, drafting. Salaries range from $15,000 for beginners and climb to nearly $40,000 for senior drafters. The average salary is between $20,000 and $25,000 a year. Use Peterson's *Two-Year Colleges* guide to find appropriate community colleges and technical institutes. The National Association of Trade and Technical Schools— P.O. Box 10429, Rockville, MD 20850—has a list of accredited private trade schools which teach drafting.

Engineering technicians

This is an exciting profession for the mechanically gifted with aptitudes in math and science, and it requires only an associate degree from a technical institute or community college. Be extremely cautious about selecting the right education for this field, however. Contact JETS, 1420 King Street, Alexandria, VA 22314 for more information. The work of engineering technicians pays between $14,000 and $40,000 a year and involves assisting engineers and scientists in government and industry research and development. Engineering technicians set up experiments, help develop new products and solve customer problems with equipment ranging from production machinery to NASA missiles, space shuttles and satellites.

Legal assistants (paralegals)

Although many employers prefer training their own legal assistants, formal training programs for paralegals are available to high school graduates at community and junior colleges, four-year colleges, trade schools and legal assistant associations. Lists of approved legal assistant training programs, career information and job opportunities are available from these organizations:

Legal Assistant Management Association, P.O. Box 40129, Overland Park, KS 66204

National Association of Legal Assistants, 1601 South Main Street, Tulsa, OK 74119

National Federation of Paralegal Associations, 104 Wilmot Road, Deerfield, IL 60015-5195

National Paralegal Association, P.O. Box 406, Solebury, PA 18963

Standing Committee on Legal Assistants, American Bar Association, 750 North Lake Shore Drive, Chicago, IL 60611

Depending on the area of the country and the size of the law firm or employer, legal assistants earn just under $20,000 a year to start and about $25,000 after three to five years experience.

Library technicians
Library technical assistants, as they're often called, perform all the support activities of a library. They help librarians prepare, organize and catalog materials; help the public; operate audio-visual equipment; organize exhibits and help clients with microfiche equipment and computers. Library technicians need a two-year community college associate degree in library technology. Salaries vary widely but average just under $20,000. It's important for you to know, however, that credits earned for an associate degree in library technology *do not* apply toward a degree in library science, which is a four-year professional degree from a college or university in preparation for a job as a librarian. For more information write to the American Library Association, Office for Library Personnel Resources, 50 East Huron Street Chicago, IL 60611.

Science technicians
For those with an interest in science, this profession offers the opportunity to work in research and development in the chemical, petroleum and food processing industries as well as in college, university and government research laboratories and the labs of research and development firms. Most junior and community colleges offer

two-year associate degrees in science, mathematics and specific technologies such as food technology. Earnings of science technicians range from $12,000 to $40,000 a year. For information about a career as a chemical technician in chemistry-related fields including food, contact the American Chemical Society, Education Division, Career Services, 1155 16th Street NW, Washington, DC 20036. For information about a career as a biological technician in biology-related fields, contact the American Institute of Biological Sciences, 730 11th Street NW, Washington, DC 20001.

TRANSPORTATION

Air transport
With the exception of flight crews, most airline and ground service personnel (flight attendants, ground crews, and so on) and airport operations staffs need no college education, although flight attendants on international routes must know appropriate foreign languages. Most training is on-the-job in formal company training programs with earnings ranging from $15,000 to $35,000 a year. Most airlines require pilots to have two years of college and many insist on a four-year college degree. Pilots must attend a certified pilot school (for a list write to Superintendent of Documents, U.S. Government Printing Office, Washington, DC 20402) or pass a Federal Aviation Administration military competency exam if they learn to fly in the military. Pilot salaries average $80,000 and range as high as $165,000 for senior pilots on major airlines. For more information about career opportunities in air transport, write to the airlines themselves, to air transport companies such as United Parcel Service or Federal Express and to Future Aviation Professionals of America, 4959 Massachusetts Blvd., Atlanta, GA 30032.

Ground transport
 Bus drivers.   Must be 18 to 24 years old, preferably high school graduates, and, depending on state regulations, have a commercial driver's license or special schoolbus license. In addition, intercity bus drivers must meet state or U.S. Department of Transportation qualifications. Training is on-the-job in formal company or transit system training programs lasting two to eight weeks. Drivers in local transit systems earn between $15,000 and $20,000 a year and

advance to $20,000 and $25,000 within five years. Experienced intercity bus drivers can earn more than $30,000 a year.

Truck drivers. Qualifications vary widely depending on the types of trucks and where goods will be carried. In general, truck drivers need to be in good physical condition and at least 21 years old to engage in interstate commerce. They must have a commercial motor vehicle operator license and take written examinations on the Motor Carrier Safety Regulations of the U.S. Department of Transportation. Many firms won't hire new drivers under 25 years old because of insurance costs. Local drivers are paid by the hour, but wages vary from community to community and whether drivers are unionized. Average income ranges from $8 an hour for driving light trucks to more than $12 an hour for driving tractor trailers. Long-distance tractor-trailer drivers, most of whom belong to the International Brotherhood of Teamsters (union), earn from $20,000 to more than $50,000 a year. For more information, write to American Trucking Associations, Inc., 2200 Mill Road, Alexandria, VA 22314 and to the Professional Truck Driver Institute of America, 8788 Elk Grove Blvd., Elk Grove, CA 95624.

Other transportation industry opportunities

- Shipping. Seamen on ocean-going vessels; mates aboard coastal and inland ships, boats and barges.
- Railroads. Locomotive engineers; brake, signal and switch operators; conductors; yard masters; yard equipment operators.
- Surface transport. Taxi drivers and chauffeurs; limousine drivers; hearse drivers; car delivery drivers for new car dealers; service station attendants; parking lot operators; car wash operators.

ARMED SERVICES (FOR NONMILITARY JOBS,
SEE GOVERNMENT SERVICE)

The U.S. Armed Services—the army, navy, marines and coast guard—offer millions of American men and women endless opportunities to learn a trade and serve their country at the same time. All branches require a high school diploma, and applicants must pass written examinations. Applicants must be at least 18 years old (or 17 with parental consent) and must agree contractually to serve at least two and usually three to four years. Together, the four services are the largest employers in the U.S. and offer the most job training and benefits. They offer training and work experience in nearly 2000 occupations, most of which are valuable in civilian life. Here are the jobs, in 12 broad categories, which are open to enlisted personnel (nonofficers) with no college education or previous experience. All training is on-the-job at full pay and at government expense.

1. Human services: recreation.
2. Media and public affairs: musicians, photographers, camera operators, graphic designers and illustrators and foreign language interpreters and translators.
3. Health care: medical laboratory technologists and technicians, radiologic technologists, emergency medical technicians, dental assistants, pharmaceutical assistants, sanitation specialists and veterinary assistants. Military training as a health care specialist automatically entitles a person to civilian certification.
4. Engineering, scientific and technical occupations: mapping technicians, computer programmers, air traffic controllers and radio and radar operators.
5. Administrative, clerical and functional support jobs: accounting clerks, payroll clerks, personnel clerks, computer programmers, computer operators, accounting machine operators, chaplain assistants, counseling aides, typists, word processor operators, stenographers, storekeepers and other clerical jobs.
6. Service occupations: military police, correction specialists, detectives, firefighters, food preparation and service.
7. Vehicle and machinery mechanics: maintenance and repair of aircraft, missiles, conventional and nuclear powered ships, boats and landing craft, trucks, earth moving equipment, armored vehicles and cars.
8. Electronic and electric repair: repairs of radio, navigation and flight control equipment, telephones, teletype and data processing equipment.
9. Construction trades: carpenters, construction and earthmoving equipment operators, metalworkers, machinists, plumbers, electricians, heating and air-

conditioning specialists and every other building trades
occupation related to construction and maintenance of
buildings, roads, bridges and airstrips.

10. Machine operating and precision work: laboratory
technicians, opticians, machinists, welders and shipfitters.

11. Transportation and materials handling: truck drivers;
aircrews; seamen; warehousing and equipment handling
specialists and all jobs associated with the operation of
transportation equipment, including trucks, ships, boats,
airplanes and helicopters; and maintaining inventories of all
spare parts.

12. Infantry, gun crews and seamen specialists: the one area
with few applications to civilian life, although some
munitions experts find work in law enforcement and
demolition, while seamen specialists often find jobs on
merchant and passenger vessels.

Enlistment is a contract in which *you* specify the occupational areas
that interest you most and in which you want to be trained before
you join. You can also apply for Officer Candidate School, and if
accepted, become an officer trained in managerial and administrative
skills. Service in the military entitles you to scholarship funds to attend college while you're in the military or after discharge. Although
the military can be a stepping stone to a rewarding civilian career, it
is also a rewarding career in itself and should be considered seriously
as such. Aside from pride of service, the military offers the most
benefits and job security of any U.S. employer. Enlisted personnel
earn an average of more than $20,000 a year in take-home pay and
housing and subsistence (food) allowances. Cash income ranges from
$646 to $864 a month along with free room and board (or a housing
and subsistence allowance), free medical and dental care, a military
clothing allowance, free on-base recreational facilities and 30 days
paid vacation a year. Warrant officer earnings average nearly $35,000
a year and commissioned officers average more than $43,000 a year
in cash and equivalents. Military personnel are eligible for retirement
benefits after only 20 years of service, including a pension worth
40% of base (cash) pay. Any veteran with two or more years of
service is eligible for free medical care at any veterans administration
hospital. For information on military careers, write to:

Department of the Army, HQUS Recruiting Command, Fort
Sheridan, IL 60037

USAF Recruiting Service, Randolph Air Force Base, TX 78150

Commandant of the Marine Corps, Headquarters, Washington,
DC 20380

Navy Recruiting Command, 4015 Wilson Blvd., Arlington, VA
22203-1991

Commandant, G-PRJ, U.S. Coast Guard, Washington, DC 20590

Chapter 4

Getting Started in Your New Career

Once you've selected the industry and career that interests you most and you've completed your alternative education for that career, you'll have to get a job. If you attended a cooperative education program, it's likely that the employer that helped train you will offer you a permanent job. In that case, you're all set. Good luck in your new job.

If you did not participate in such a program, but carefully evaluated the one you did attend and picked a good one, that program's job placement service will put you in touch with employers looking for your skills. You'll also want to contact employers on your own. With or without help from others, the job of getting a job is simple. It will take time; it may be frustrating; but the techniques are simple. Don't complicate them and don't let others complicate them or discourage you. Many friends and relatives will tell you "you're doing it all wrong" and flood you with endless articles and books about "How to Get a Good Job" and "How to Write a Good Resume." Chances are all those articles and books contain good pointers, but you may find yourself spending more time reading about how to get a job instead of going out and getting one.

The principles in all those books and articles are the same. Identify your skills and positive traits, get them down on paper in summary or *resume* form and get that resume into the hands of the one employer in ten or one hundred or one thousand who is looking for your combination of skills and personality.

Writing Resumes

A resume is not an autobiography. It is a *sales pitch*—a written advertisement of skills and services for sale. It's the reverse of a help wanted ad. A help wanted ad never tells you any negatives about a job, only the positives. Like all ads, it's a teaser, which lures readers into contacting the employer to get more details. Which of these ads would tease you into making a call to get more details?

Administrative Assistant: Top salary, flexible hours, interesting, congenial atmosphere on TV talk show team. Must be able to handle contacts with guest personalities. Call 555-0000.

Secretary: Take dictation (80 words/min), type letters, file documents, answer telephones, carry messages, run errands for busy executive. Hours 9 to 5, five days a week, but must be ready to work evenings and some weekends. Salary: $18,000. Call XYZ Productions. . . .

The two jobs are identical, but the top ad makes it more attractive by keeping details to a minimum and only listing positive aspects of the job. And that's what you've got to do with your resume. Every job has negative characteristics, but the ad that features them will get no takers. The same is true for resumes. We all have have our weaknesses, but they don't go in our resumes. Similarly, too many details can destroy the value of an ad by discouraging a response from an applicant who doesn't fit the job perfectly—the otherwise perfect candidate who can only take dictation at 60 words a minute, for example. That candidate might respond to the first ad but not the second, and the company would be the loser by not even getting a chance to interview the perfect candidate.

These same rules apply to resumes. Once again, a resume is not your life history. It is an ad, a sales promotion piece. Keep it short (no more than one page); keep it simple; keep it positive; and, as in all ads, show its readers how your skills and services can so benefit them that they'll invite you for an interview. And that's what your resume is for—to get you an invitation for an interview. Don't misunderstand its purpose: A resume will usually not get you a job, only a job interview.

A resume has two elements: form and content. There are simple rules for both. Break these rules and your prospective employer will assume you cannot follow any rules. Your resume will end up in a special file for rejected applications—the waste basket. The important thing to keep in mind in writing a resume is that it is one of the few aspects in the job application process that is totally under your control. You cannot control job market conditions or the quality of other applicants competing with you. But you can control what goes into your resume.

Here are the rules for resume form:

1. **Brevity.** *No more than one page long.* An inability to reduce a resume to one page shows either a lack of command of the English language, an inability to follow directions or an inflated sense of self-importance—none of which are characteristics that employers admire.

2. **Neatness.** Absolute perfection is the rule. There is no excuse for not being able to produce a perfect resume in the quiet and privacy of one's home away from all pressures. If you can't produce an absolutely neat one-page paper, potential employers will assume you can't do anything neatly.

3. **Factual accuracy.** Potential employers will check the facts in your resume. Be certain they are accurate. If they're not, a potential employer will conclude that you are either dishonest or unable to do accurate work.

4. **Honesty.** Don't exaggerate by calling your summer job as a file clerk an "administrative assistant." And if you cut lawns as a summer job or picked vegetables, say so. Don't call yourself a landscape or agricultural technician.

5. **Writing accuracy.** Your resume must be free of spelling, grammatical and typographical errors. Again, if you can't produce a one-page paper free of errors, employers will conclude you can't do any error-free work.

6. **Personal data.** You should not include a photograph of yourself or personal information such as height, weight, sex, race or religion. It is against state and federal law to mention any characteristics associated with discrimination based on race, religion or gender.

7. **Standard presentation.** Don't use off-sized or off-color paper. You are writing for businesspeople. Be businesslike. Use standard 8½-in. × 11-in. white paper. Artistic attention-getting devices, which parents and teachers may have thought cute or even imaginative in school, will only be tossed away as unbusinesslike by potential employers.

8. **Well organized.** The resume should be organized into four or five basic categories, that is, each headed by a capitalized or underlined heading. There are three basic methods of organization: chronological (in order of occurrence), functional (in order of importance)

and combined chronological and functional. The last format is usually the most effective and the one used in the following sample. It orders the broad categories by importance for the job you're applying for, but orders the information within each category chronologically, either backwards or forwards, depending on which is more effective.

9. **Typography.** Resumes should be typed and printed or copied on print-quality dry copying machines or prepared on a letter-quality word processor. Do not use a dot matrix printer, and never send a carbon copy! Word processing is by far the most preferable, because it allows you to use a basic format, which you can adapt slightly or "custom design" for each prospective employer. Someone interested in a secretarial career might want to modify the objective to read "Secretarial work in health care field" for one prospective employer and "Secretarial work, scientific research" for another. In other words, you can show a specific interest in a particular company. That's almost impossible with a printed resume, whose tone must be general enough to send to a wide variety of prospective employers. It says the same thing to every company and shows no particular interest in any.

Here are the rules for content, followed by a sample resume on page 108, which you can use by substituting your own data for the fictitious information:

Name, address and telephone number, centered at the top of the page

Career **objective**
Notice that I've used the word *career* rather than occupational or job objective. That's because by stating a broad career goal, you give a potential employer who likes your resume more flexibility than you would by stating the specific job you're seeking. If you list bartending as a job objective, for example, and there are better, more experienced applicants, you'll be rejected. But if you list restaurant and hotel service, the same employer who might reject you for the bartender's job may be eager to give you some other opportunity as a waiter or assistant host if your training warrants it. Similarly, the modest applicant who specifies "entry level position in public relations" may get no job at all (because there is no entry-level job) or he might win that entry-level job and miss getting a better job for

which his resume kept him from being considered. If you specify an entry-level job, that's all you'll probably be considered for. So, again, don't close doors of opportunity on yourself by narrowing your goals or being unnecessarily modest.

Job qualifications

The next category of data should tell the employer that you know how to do the job he has. If you've just graduated from school and learned those skills in a vocational education program, you should put "Education" as the next category in your resume. If, on the other hand, you learned most of the skills you need through previous work experience, then "Work Experience" should be next. Within the category of job qualifications, list each experience chronologically, with the most recent one first. With each experience, indicate *briefly* what skill you learned or used that will be of value to your prospective employer. Also mention any special award or accomplishment associated with each experience. Whether you're submitting your resume to a giant corporation or a local grocery store, prospective employers want to know the same thing: that you can do the job they're trying to fill. You can demonstrate that to them by showing that you either learned how at a good vocational school or that you've actually done it on-the-job.

References

List the names, addresses and telephone numbers of former employers or teachers who had key roles in teaching you the skills needed for the job you're applying for. There's no point listing a 9th-grade teacher who likes you a lot. The only teachers you should consider are those who taught you your trade and, perhaps, the director of the program in which you learned that trade.

Optional categories

Special skills. If you're fluent in a foreign language or have some other special skill or knowledge not mentioned under "Experience"—it could be a hobby or travel experience—that might prove *useful* to your employer, mention it under this listing. Remember: It must prove useful, not just interesting.

Awards and affiliations. If you've won an award or have some position in a club or organization where you display other talents your employer could use, then add this category to your resume. An example might be, "Treasurer, Smithville Boys Club. Managed membership dues collections, club solicitations, investments and disbursements and maintained accounts ledgers." Such an example shows your familiarity with handling and managing organization funds and with accounting and bookkeeping. It also reflects a community's faith in your honesty and trustworthiness. It displays another positive element of your character in just a few words, without any bragging or exaggeration.

Writing style
Keep each statement short. Do not use complete sentences such as, "I worked as a salesperson behind the greeting card counter." Instead, the description of such a previous job should read, "Salesperson, greeting cards. Actively managed customer sales, cash flow, inventory controls, reorders of 16 product lines from five vendors." And, if your work was particularly notable, you would add to the description, "Salesperson of the Month Award, December 1990," or "Reorganized inventory controls to reduce perennial shrinkage from 3.24% of purchasing costs to 0.14% with annual savings of $46,542 to the department."

There are two other important elements in a good resume writing style. One is the use of active, meaningful verbs to describe what you did on the job or learned in the classroom—for example, "reorganized" rather than "changed" or "managed" rather than "responsible for." Be careful *not* to write a job description, only what you did on the job and only those accomplishments that might be of use to your new employer. Follow each job title with an action verb: "introduced," "inspected," "maintained," "prepared," "organized," "controlled," "planned," "initiated," "executed," "analyzed," "documented," "designed," "monitored," "modified," "systematized," "streamlined," "converted," "promoted" and so on. In describing classroom training experiences, use the phrase "hands-on operation" or "hands-on production" to indicate you actually operated some equipment or produced some product.

The other important element in a good writing style is the avoidance of jargon, which is a wordy, meaningless phrase for which a single word can be substituted. Our daily speech is filled with jargon: "at this point in time" instead of "now"; "at some future point in time" instead of "soon"; "in order to" or "for the purpose of" or "with a view toward" instead of "to"; "with respect to" instead of "about." In other words, keep your sentences short and to the point.

Figure 2 on page 108 is a sample resume in which the job applicant is seeking a career in merchandising, or retailing. He has learned his skills both in college and working at summer jobs. Had he majored in English instead of marketing, his work experience would have been listed first. But the broad nature of his business education warrants its appearance before his work experience, which, after all, was only summer work and probably did not give him the in-depth understanding of retail operations that he studied in college. Had this been a resume of a young man who had graduated two years earlier and then worked for two years in a department store, his work experience would have been listed before his education.

The resume is purposely "average"—no awards, no super achievements—because most of us are average. The trick to resume writing is to display the solidity, dependability and skills that someone with an average background and education can develop. Notice, too, how the resume can be used to match individual employer needs with as little as a single word change. As it stands, it is a valid resume for any department store. But, if he changed his career goal from "Merchandising" to "Fashion Merchandising" or "Merchandising, Menswear," it would be a particularly effective resume for any menswear retailer. By leaving his career objective as it is, however, and by expanding his experience in the student book store, he could send his resume to any store that sells student supplies in or near a college or university.

The Cover Letter

In some cases, you hand-deliver your resume to a prospective employer. Every resume that's sent by mail, however, should have a cover letter regardless of how you made initial contact with a prospective employer. Just as the resume is designed to get you an interview, the cover letter is designed to get the recipient to read your resume. The cover letter, therefore, is not a rehash of your resume. It must be different. Like the resume, it must be a teaser and intrigue its reader to look at the enclosed resume.

Eugene Everett Richards
687 Saybrook Court
Yalesville, CT 10101
Tel: (718) 563–4839

CAREER
OBJECTIVE: Merchandising

EDUCATION: Rockdale Community College, Associate Degree, Marketing, June 1992. Courses: Accounting, Retail Computer Applications, Marketing, Merchandising, Store Management.

Rockdale High School. Graduated, June 1990 with honors. Academic Program with marketing and accounting electives.

WORK
EXPERIENCE: September 1991 – May 1992. Hands–on management (as part of ''Store Management'' course), RCC Student Book Store: purchasing, pricing, inventory controls, reorder of books and student supplies including stationery, toiletries and college souvenir clothing; employee relations.

Summer 1991. Salesman, men's furnishings (shirts, socks, underwear, handkerchiefs). Active selling: Guided customer selection with emphasis on sales of latest, high mark–up designer brands and fashionwear; processed all aspects of sales transactions.

Summer 1990. Stock clerk, men's apparel. Managed restocking of floor racks and shelves with suits, sport shirts, dress shirts, socks, underwear and other furnishings; processed automatic reorders via computer terminals.

Binghamton Department Store, summers, 1990, 1991.

SPECIAL
SKILLS: Fluent in conversational and commercial Spanish.

REFERENCES: Mr. Donald Director
President
Binghamton Department Store
321 Downtown Mall
Binghamton, NJ 07698

Dr. Emma Educator
President
Rockdale Community College
876 Wisdom Road
Rockdale, NY 10893

Figure 2.   Sample resume of a graduating community college student.

The principles of resume writing apply to the cover letter. It must be short (one page only), neat, accurate, free of spelling, grammatical and typographical errors and prepared on a typewriter or letter-quality word processor on standard paper or stationery in standard business-letter format, as in the following sample. If you have business-type stationery with your own letterhead, use it. Otherwise, type your letterhead in the upper right hand corner. Do not use small or decoratively printed personal stationery. Again, avoid cuteness such as "Hi!" or a pompous attitude, such as "Here's the letter you've been waiting for!" As in the case of the resume, the cover letter is another aspect of keeping the job application process completely under your control. Produce a letter that will make you a desirable candidate.

You are writing to conservative businesspeople who have one goal— to improve company operations. Your letter must be conservative and businesslike and indicate that you can make a contribution to the company. You can use the sample letter on page 110 by substituting the facts of your own background for those of the fictitious job applicant.

In general, a cover letter should be no longer than three paragraphs, preferably two. You must make three points:

1. Why you are writing. Although the saying, "It's not what you know, it's who you know" doesn't always apply, contacts often can be important factors in getting a job. If you get the job, of course, you'll have to prove yourself, and contacts won't help you much. But for getting that first chance, the person with contacts and good references will usually win out over the applicant without them, all other things being equal. So, your opening sentence in any cover letter should mention your contact, if you have one, and his or her connection to either the company or to you. The contact may be a friend of the person you're writing; an official in the company; the job placement counselor at your school or college; a teacher or official at your college or school; an employment agent or a parent or relative. Whoever the contact, if you have one, use it—and use it to begin your opening sentence. Don't waste time: play your strong cards immediately.

"Ms. Doris Manning, vice-president of marketing, suggested I write to you . . ." or "My father, Samuel Richards, an attorney at . . ." or "Dr. Frederick Walker, president of Rockdale Community Col-

Eugene Everett Richards
687 Saybrook Court
Yalesville, CT 10101
May 1, 19xx

Ms. Cherie Lorraine
Director
Executive Training Program
Smith's Department Store
Barclay Square
New York, NY 10036

Dear Ms. Lorraine:

Mr. Donald Director, president of Binghamton Department
Store, suggested I write to you to apply to Smith's Executive
Training Program. As you can see in my enclosed resume, I
will be graduating from Rockdale Community College this June
with an Associate Degree in Marketing. As part of my course
in store management, I had the opportunity to participate in
hands-on management of the Rockdale Community College book-
store. Together with my two summers as a stock clerk and then
a salesperson in men's furnishings at Binghamton Department
Store, my work in merchandising—especially with goods designed for younger men and women—has proved the most exciting experience in my life. I want to make it my career, and I
would love to work at Smith's.

I would be most grateful for the opportunity of an interview
with you to see if you think I might qualify for Smith's Executive Training Program.

With many thanks for your consideration.

Sincerely,

Eugene Everett Richards

lege . . ." or "Mrs. Patricia Lane of the Rockdale Community College Job Placement Office, suggested I write you . . .".

If you do not have a contact, explain what motivated the letter: "I
saw your advertisement . . ." or, if you contacted the company "cold"
by telephone, "I enjoyed talking with you today about the possibility
of my working at . . .".

Once you've explained who or what put you in touch with the company, finish the opening by explaining the reason for writing: "... about the opening for a salesperson in the Smith's Menswear Department" or "about an opening in the Smith's Executive Training Program" or "about the possibility of a job in merchandising at Smith's."

2. Who you are. Again, keep this short. You're either a graduate of or will soon graduate from a school or college where you studied some courses or trade important in the job you're applying for. In one sentence say why you want to make that trade your career and why you want to work at the company you're writing to. Those two short sentences are probably the most difficult sentences any job applicant ever has to write. They sound simple enough, but they're not. They require considerable soul searching and research—but you must do it. Anyone who eventually hires you will want to know why you want to go into your chosen field and why you want to work for that particular company. So, you might just as well pinpoint the reasons now. And if you can't figure out the reasons, perhaps you're going into the wrong trade or applying for a job at the wrong company. The way to get started is to list all the characteristics you like about the trade you've chosen. Then reword those characteristics to have more meaning for others who may be unfamiliar with that industry. Take the fictitious job applicant in the preceding letter who obviously likes working in stores. Why would anyone want to spend eight to ten hours a day on his feet five or six days a week listening to complaining customers? Well, those who make a career out of and love merchandising don't see those as negative aspects. They see the positiveness—the excitement of facilitating the huge flow of goods from manufacturer to consumer. They enjoy the satisfaction of filling consumer needs, of discovering new products, of setting new fashion trends. They see themselves, to paraphrase a General Electric Co. advertising slogan, bringing good things to their community and its people.

In the interview, which follows, you'll have to explain in detail why you like the trade you've chosen. For the second sentence of your cover letter, however, you must summarize it in one line, as the fictitious applicant has done: "... merchandising ... goods designed for younger men and women has proved the most exciting experience in my life.'' And in the next line, explain why you want to work for that company. Your reasons may have to do with the company's standing in the community, in the industry or in the nation or your own experience with its products or services. They cannot be trivial or selfish. Just because you can walk to work is not a good primary reason. It's a good secondary reason, which you can bring up in the interview. After all, proximity to your work is valuable to your employer as well as to you, because it reduces employee lateness and absenteeism. But proximity cannot be a reason to put in your cover letter. It's essential to research the reasons for wanting to work for a company. Get an annual report to shareholders; study company brochures about its operations and its products and services; and speak to current and former employees and to customers. You may find you don't want to work for that company. But if you do, tell them why in one short sentence of your cover letter.

3. What you want the reader to do. Obviously, you want the reader of your letter to read your resume and interview you for a job. Say so quickly and politely at the end of your cover letter, as the applicant has done in the sample. You may use any acceptable sign-off: "Sincerely," "Sincerely yours" or "Yours truly."

Do not enclose any other material—only your resume and a cover letter. If you have any supporting materials, such as letters of recommendation or charts or spreadsheets that show the kind and quality of work you did, bring those with you to the interview. Never send them by mail unless you are specifically requested to do so and then include a self-addressed, stamped envelope for their return.

The Personal Interview

As in the case of the resume and cover letter, the personal interview is another aspect of the job application package under your control. It is an opportunity for you to display a depth of knowledge and aspects of your personality that dry facts and statistics on an application or resume cannot exhibit. The interview—sometimes there may be a series of two or three for the job you're seeking—is the final stage of your quest for employment. Do well in it, and you'll probably be hired.

The Interview Guidelines on page 116 lists the range of questions interviewers at one large U.S. corporation asks job applicants. The forms they use show you exactly how they handle the entire interview process. As you can see, the first thing interviewers look for is the applicant's appearance. So do enough advance research to determine the proper dress for the job you're trying to get. If people who hold similar jobs normally wear dresses or ties and jackets, then you must do so also. A company is not like school where the person who stands out in the crowd because of unusual conduct or dress will win some admiration. The interview is the moment to prove you can be part of the company's team and play by the company's rules. In addition to dress, posture and grooming are important elements of everyone's appearance. Slouching in one's seat can cost an applicant a job. Failure to look the interviewer in the eye, nervous habits and any other unusual behavior can all go down as negatives in an application folder.

Interviewers will note both the manners and language of applicants. The repetitive use of the word *like* and the phrase "ya know," as in "Like . . . ya know . . ." will certainly produce negative reactions from interviewers. So will responses such as "Cool!" and immature speech patterns such as, "Well, ya know, I kinda like computers, ya know, and, uh, like, ya know, electronic equipment and, ya know . . ." Clear, effective communication is important in every job involving other people. Everyone on the team has to be able to understand what other team members say and write. An applicant who has not yet learned how to communicate effectively will find it difficult to get a good job, because most employers seek applicants who have the ability to articulate well.

One-word answers also leave interviewers unimpressed and hurt any chances of getting a job—as it did this applicant, whose interview began this way:

Interviewer: Did you find your way here all right?
Applicant: Yeah.
Interviewer: No trouble at all, eh?

Applicant: Nah.
Interviewer: Well, have a seat.
Applicant sits without replying.
Interviewer: Let's see . . . you're applying for the sales job in
          menswear, right?
Applicant: Yeah.

Although such answers may be the result of shyness, they usually appear to others as unfriendly and rude. The ability to engage in conversation is always seen as a sign of good manners and friendliness.

Another error that can earn a job rejection is poor grammar, especially for office jobs. A lot of poor grammar such as "Things are going good" instead of "well" or "Me and my friends went to the movies" instead of "My friends and I . . ." may be the result of bad habits, not lack of knowledge. If that's the case for you, begin changing those habits in your everyday speech now before you begin the round of job interviews. Poor grammar can hurt your chances of getting a good job, and it can affect your entire career.

In addition to proper conduct, dress and speech, it's important to go into an interview knowing as much about a particular company as possible. Almost every interviewer will ask why you want to work for his or her company, and it's important that you know why, specifically, on the basis of your in-depth reading of its annual report, sales brochures, product catalogs and any other printed materials. Most major libraries carry directories of corporations—*Moody's,* for example, or *Standard & Poor's,* or *Value Line*—that contain much data about all major companies. When an interviewer asks what you know about the company, you should know more than "just what I read in the newspapers." Your answer should demonstrate initiative and interest. You should know its history, the products and services it offers and something about its top officials. You should know what makes the company unique and exactly why you want to work for it. An applicant who doesn't know why he or she wants a job at a particular company should not be there in the first place. Even if the real reason is because you need a job and are willing to take anything you can get, don't say so. You'll probably never get work that way. Nor are you likely to get a job by saying that your friends work there, and they say, "It's a nice place."

Remember that most interviewers are probably quite proud of their companies. They see their firms as unique, and they see the job you're applying for as a unique opportunity. Do enough research to find out what makes each firm unique and why the job you're after is indeed a great opportunity for you. If you don't see it as such, perhaps you should consider waiting for a better opportunity.

In addition to knowing as much as possible about the company and the job, it's important to know all about yourself. Remember that the interview represents a common measuring stick for all applicants— no matter what schools or colleges they attended; no matter what contacts they have; no matter what previous jobs they've held and no matter what their social backgrounds. Everybody walks into the interview facing the same test. Whether you're shy or outgoing, the interview is something you'll have to face all your life. It's a chance to sell yourself. Use it to good advantage. If you're not skilled at having interviews, practice with friends or family. Have them ask you questions. The following is a list of typical questions asked by professional job interviewers. Rehearse your entrance into the interviewer's office. Walk into the room with quiet self-confidence, smiling and looking him or her straight in the eye and firmly shaking hands. Rehearse your exit: shaking hands again, saying thanks for the interview, then turning and walking out, again with quiet self-confidence. Rehearse often. Move the furniture around in a room at home to make a stage set of an interviewer's office with a desk or table in the middle, you on one side and a friend or relative on the other.

Interview techniques vary widely from company to company and interviewer to interviewer. Some interviewers may be as new at it— and as nervous—as you. You might even be the first person they have ever interviewed. Most personnel executives, however, are quite skilled. Some will purposely make the situation more stressful for you than others to see how you respond to pressures. Typical stress interviews begin with such questions such as, "What can I do for you?" or "Tell me about yourself"; "What kind of job are you looking for?"; "Why do you think you're the right person for this job?"; "What do you know about the job (or company or 'me,' if

INTERVIEW GUIDELINES

Here is the full range of questions most good interviewers will ask job applicants. Can you answer the ones appropriate for your background and the type of job you're seeking? If not, start practicing. There are three sections to the interview package. The first section lists a range of questions to ask. The second section tells the interviewer what to listen and look for—especially appearance, manner, self-expression and responsiveness on the part of the applicant. And the third section asks the interviewer to rate the applicant on appearance, work experience, education and present activities and interests—and then recommend for or against hiring. Use this material to help you prepare for your interviews.

Outlined below are the four major areas of the applicant that you should investigate: Work Experience, Education and Training, Goals and Ambitions, and Self-Assessment. The questions within each area are suggested topics for you to explore. Ask these questions in your own words and style, and add any questions you feel necessary within each category. Be sure to cover each area thoroughly. Remember, the following are only sample questions and are, by no means, an exhaustive list.

Work Experience

1. Please describe your present responsibilities and duties.
2. What were some of the things that you particularly enjoyed when you were working for the ABC Corporation?
3. What do you consider to have been your chief accomplishments at ABC Corporation?
4. Tell me about the personal progress that you made during your association with the ABC Corporation.
5. Looking back at the time spent with the ABC Corporation, what do you feel you have gained from your association?
6. What were your reasons for leaving the ABC Corporation?
7. In the past, for what things have your superiors complimented you? For what have they criticized you?
8. What were some of the problems that you encountered on your job and how did you solve these problems?
9. As you see it, what would be some advantages to you were you to join our company? What disadvantages or drawbacks might there be?
10. Describe a typical day on your last job.

Education

1. How did you select the college you attended?
2. What did you hope to do with your education?
3. How do you think college contributed to your development?
4. How would you describe your academic achievement?
5. Have you had any additional training or education since graduating college?
6. Looking back at your college education, how do you feel it has prepared you for a position as a _____?
7. How did you select your major course of study?

Goals and Ambitions

1. What are you looking for in a job?
2. Why does this job sound appealing to you?
3. What would you like to be doing in 3 years?   5 years?
4. What would you want in your next job that you are not getting now?
5. What are some of the things in a job that are important to you?
6. In considering joining a company, what are some of the factors that you take into account?
7. What are your present salary expectations?

Self-Assessment

1. In general, how would you describe yourself?
2. What do you regard to be your outstanding qualities?
3. Why have you progressed to where you are?
4. What kinds of situations in circumstances make you feel tense or nervous?
5. In which areas do you feel you would like to develop yourself?
6. What do you feel you have to offer us?
7. We all have our strengths and weaknesses. What do you feel are your greatest strengths, and what are those areas that you would like to improve upon?

Keep Questions Open-Ended

Introduction		
Cover: Greeting Small talk Opening ques- tion Lead question		Look for: Appearance Manner Self-expression Responsiveness

Work Experience		
Cover: Earliest jobs, part-time, tem- porary Military assign- ments Full-time posi- tions	Ask: Things done best? Done less well? Things liked best? Liked less well? Major accomplishments? How achieved? Most difficult problems faced? How handled? Ways most effective with people? Ways less effective? Level of earnings? Reasons for changing jobs? What learned from work experience? What looking for in job? In career?	Look for: Relevance of work Sufficiency of work Skill and competence Adaptability Productivity Motivation Interpersonal relations Leadership Growth and develop- ment

Education		
Cover: Elementary school High school College Specialized train- ing Recent courses	Ask: Best subjects? Subjects done less well? Subject liked most? Liked least? Reactions to teachers? Level of grades? Effort required? Reasons for choosing school? Major field? Special achievements?	Look for: Relevance of school- ing Sufficiency of school- ing Intellectual abilities Versatility Breadth and depth of knowledge Level of accomplish- ment

	Toughest problems? Role in extracurricular activities? How financed educa- tion? Relation of education to career? Consider further school- ing?	Motivation, interests Reaction to authority Leadership Team work

Summary

Cover:
Strengths
Weaknesses
	Ask:
	What bring to job?
	   What are assets?
	What are best talents?
	What qualities seen by
	   self or others?
	What makes you good
	   investment for em-
	   ployer?
	What are shortcomings?
	What areas need im-
	   provement?
	What qualities wish to
	   develop further?
	What constructive criti-
	   cism from others?
	How might you be risk
	   for employer?
	What further training, or
	   experience, might you
	   need?
		Look for:
		PLUS (+) AND
		   MINUS (−)
		Talents, skills
		Knowledge
		Energy
		Motivation
		Interests
		Personal qualities
		Social qualities
		Character
		Situational factors

Closing remarks

Cover:
Comments regarding interview
   and applicant
Further contacts to be made
Course of action to be taken
Cordial parting

Applicant: _____ Date: _____

Position: _____

Interviewer: _____

Comment on the applicant's background and behavior, taking into consideration the elements listed in the right-hand column of each section.
Then circle a rating for each section based on the evidence you have
cited. Finally, at the end of this report, make one overall rating of the
candidate.

Initial Impression
Manner Self-expression Responsiveness Favorable 1 2 3 4 5 Unfavorable
Work Experience
Relevance of work Sufficiency of work Skill and competence Adaptability Productivity Motivation Interpersonal relations Leadership Growth and development Favorable 1 2 3 4 5 Unfavorable
Education
Relevance of schooling Sufficiency of schooling Intellectual abilities Versatility Breadth and depth of knowl- edge Level of accomplishment Motivation, interests Reaction to authority Leadership Team work Favorable 1 2 3 4 5 Unfavorable

Present Activities and Interests

Maturity and judgment
Intellectual growth
Diversity of interests
Social skills
Leadership

Favorable 1 2 3 4 5 Unfavorable

Summary of Strengths (+)	Summary of Weaknesses (−)

Overall Summary Recommendations (write three paragraphs)

1. In favor of hiring: _____

2. Against hiring: _____

3. Final recommendation: _____

4. Overall Rating:
   Favorable 1 2 3 4 5 Unfavorable

Thank you for your feedback. Please forward to Personnel.

the interviewer is your prospective boss)?''; ''Where else are you looking?''; ''Why did you leave your last job?''; ''What did you like least about your last job?''; ''Can you work under extreme pressure?'' These are all tough questions, and you should be prepared for them in advance by thinking them through carefully and having a specific, direct answer—nothing vague.

Remember that you are there to describe your qualifications for the job. Don't let yourself get side-tracked. Answer the stressful questions, but immediately steer the conversation back to your skills. *Don't* focus on the stresses of the situation but on the reason for being there: to display the elements of your background, character, education, skills and personality that make you uniquely qualified for the job you're applying for.

Most interviewers will begin with a series of random questions to try to put you at ease. They'll find some topic that will get you talking comfortably so that you'll relax enough to talk openly and honestly about yourself. Good interviewers want applicants to do most of the talking during the 30 to 45 minutes of the interview so that they can get an idea of the applicant's personality and the way they think.

Before going into an interview, it's important to make a careful assessment of all those characteristics that qualify you for the job. Write them on a list in order of importance, and learn them so well that you can discuss your life and talents in any order—either in piecemeal answers to many questions or in an interesting discourse in answer to a single, general question such as, "Tell me about yourself." And don't be afraid to take notes with you. It's perfectly acceptable to refer to them during the interview. Try to know them by heart, of course, but don't be afraid to pause and look at them and say, "I just want to make sure I've covered everything." Be sure that you talk about your qualifications for the job. Describe specific, concrete examples of what you've done either in the classroom, school laboratory or on some other job that demonstrate your ability to do the job you're applying for and to fulfill the company's needs.

Take a notepad and pencil. It's important to listen to what your interviewer has to say and to demonstrate that you are a good listener and interested enough to take notes on what you consider essential information.

Notes are also helpful for questioning your interviewer. "Do you have any questions?" is a question almost every interviewer will ask—and you'd better have some or risk a poor score on your interview. One important one is to get an outline of the responsibilities of the job you're seeking. Some other obvious questions are, "What kind of person are you looking for?" "Why did the last person leave this job?" or "Where might this job lead, if I do very well?" Some better ones would be, "How would you like to see the work done on this job? Has it been done that way? How would you like to see it improved? What's a typical day on the job like? What's the best thing about the job? The worst thing? What are some of the problems I'll face on the job?" On a broader level, your reading about the company might produce these questions: "I read in the papers that sales are (slipping) (growing). Does this mean the company might (cut back) (expand) operations? Would this job (be in jeopardy) (have more responsibilities)?"

Another type of question to ask, depending on the interviewer's personality, is the interviewer's own experiences and length of service at the company. "How long have you been here, and what do you see as the strengths and weaknesses of the company?" Remember, the word "interview" means "to see one another." Most people think it means one person questioning another, but the original meaning is for two people to see each other. Use the situation to establish a rapport with your interviewer and get a friendly, two-way conversation going. If you think the offices are beautiful, say so; if the building or factory is impressive, say so. Conversation is an art that will certainly help you score well in any interview situation.

Write your questions down in advance, and don't be afraid when the time comes to say, "Yes. I wrote a few down," and then refer to your notes.

One of the "loaded" questions most interviewers will almost certainly ask you is to tell them about your weak points. Nobody's perfect, and your interviewer knows that. You'll appear rather conceited if you say you have none, and you'll show a lack of self-knowledge if you say you don't know what they are. There are two rules for handling the problem. The first is to discuss all weak points that will ultimately surface in a check of your application facts and your references. You're far better off discussing such weaknesses in advance so that they don't come as a surprise later and force the company to reject your application. Often, by explaining some weak point at the interview, you can reduce it's importance and make it seem insignificant.

If no weak points will ever turn up in the company's check into your background and references, the way to prepare for an interviewer's question about them is to list them all before the interview at the same time you list all your strong points. Be honest with yourself. No one will see the list but you. Then cross out the worst of the weak points and save the most common, almost humorous ones that will not or cannot in any way affect your job performance. Then discuss them with a smile and show yourself to be human.

An important rule in interview techniques is never to begin or end an interview on a negative note, and, after any discussion of weak points, be certain to show how you've converted a weakness into a strength. Someone weak in high school math, for example, might well have taken a special summer school course to strengthen mathematical skills.

Another important rule at job interviews is to show that you want the job. If an interviewer doesn't think you want it, you won't get it. As in any relationship, clear communication is vital in interviews. You must tell other people what you need and want or they'll never know. So, at an appropriate point—usually, toward the end of the interview when you're asked if you have any other questions or if "there's anything else you'd like to discuss"—speak up and say something like, "I just want you to know that I'd really like to work for this company, and I'd really like this job. I think I can do a good job and make a contribution to the company." Or, if the interviewer is the person you'll actually be working for: "I'd really like to work for you. I know I can do a good job and make a contribution to your department." Don't be afraid to say things such as, "I promise you won't be sorry if you hire me" or "This job is exactly what I've been looking for—it ties in perfectly with everything I've ever learned and studied about . . ." Be enthusiastic, however, and say you want the job!

Chances are you won't get a job offer on the spot. Usually, the interviewer will tell you that the company will give your application careful consideration and that they will let you know within a few days. Regardless of how friendly or enthusiastic your interviewer may seem, keep looking for other jobs while awaiting the company's decision.

After your interview, write a thank-you letter that reinforces your interest in and qualifications for the job. Here is a sample letter:

Eugene Everett Richards
687 Saybrook Court
Yalesville, CT 10101

June 1, 19xx

Ms. Cherie Lorraine
Director
Executive Training Program
Smith's Department Store
Barclay Square
New York, NY 10036

Dear Ms. Lorraine:

It was kind of you to take so much time to see me yesterday. I enjoyed meeting you and learning so much about Smith's and the Executive Training Program. I'm even more excited now about the prospect of a career in merchandising, and there's no place I'd rather work than at Smith's. Obviously, a chance to join the Smith's Executive Training Program would be the opportunity of a lifetime, and I promise that, given that chance, I would not let you or Smith's down.

All my thanks for your consideration.

Sincerely,

Eugene Everett Richards

Don't be disappointed if you don't get the job. Remember, there is no way for you to know the qualifications of other job applicants. Moreover, many companies make mistakes, and there's nothing you can do about it except to keep applying at other companies until you find the job that's right for you at a company that's eager to have you on its team.

Filling in Applications

As in all other written work in the job application process, your application must be filled in neatly with no spelling, grammatical or typographical errors. Unlike resumes and letters, however, you probably won't be able to fill in your job application in the serenity of your home. In all likelihood, a personnel department official will give you the application and a pen or pencil and direct you to a small corner table or desk where you'll have to fill it in on the spur of the moment. So, be prepared. The following is a sample of a typical application. First, practice filling it in carefully and neatly. Make a few copies and see if you can do it error free without having to cross out or erase any entries. Next, use it to make a list of the information and vital statistics *you know* every job application will demand. There is nothing worse than having to tell the personnel office that you don't have or forgot some information about yourself—like your social security number—and that you'll telephone them later with the information. That is inefficiency of the worst kind—and usually unforgiveable, because it demonstrates what you may be like on the job. So make a list of the data required in most job applications and have it with you whenever you visit a prospective employer.

And, once again, good luck!

Figure 3. A standard employment application used by companies across the United States. Make a copy and practice filling it out neatly and *error-free*. Make a list of the data required so you have all the pertinent facts with you when you have to fill applications in actual situations.

Application
For Employment

We consider applicants for all positions without regard to race, color, religion, sex, national origin, age, marital or veteran status, the presence of a non-job-related medical condition or handicap, or any other legally protected status.

(PLEASE PRINT)

Position(s) Applied For	Date of Application

How Did You Learn About Us?

☐ Advertisement   ☐ Friend   ☐ Walk-In

☐ Employment Agency   ☐ Relative   ☐ Other _____

Last Name	First Name	Middle Name

Address Number Street	City	State	Zip Code

Telephone Number(s)	Social Security Number

If you are under 18 years of age, can you provide required proof of your eligibility to work?   ☐ Yes   ☐ No

Have you ever filed an application with us before?   ☐ Yes   ☐ No

If Yes, give date _____

Have you ever been employed with us before?   ☐ Yes   ☐ No

If Yes, give date _____

Are you currently employed?   ☐ Yes   ☐ No

May we contact your present employer?   ☐ Yes   ☐ No

Are you prevented from lawfully becoming employed in this country because of Visa or Immigration Status?   ☐ Yes   ☐ No
Proof of citizenship or immigration status will be required upon employment.

On what date would you be available for work? _____

Are you available to work: ☐ Full Time   ☐ Part Time   ☐ Shift Work   ☐ Temporary

Are you currently on "lay-off" status and subject to recall?   ☐ Yes   ☐ No

Can you travel if a job requires it?   ☐ Yes   ☐ No

Have you been convicted of a felony within the last 7 years?   ☐ Yes   ☐ No
Conviction will not necessarily disqualify an applicant from employment.

If Yes, please explain _____

WE ARE AN EQUAL OPPORTUNITY EMPLOYER

Education

	Elementary School				High School				Undergraduate College / University				Graduate / Professional			
School Name and Location																
Years Completed	4	5	6	7	8	9	10	11	12	1	2	3	4	1	2	3	4
Diploma / Degree																
Describe Course of Study																
Describe any specialized training, apprenticeship, skills and extra-curricular activities																
Describe any honors you have received																
State any additional information you feel may be helpful to us in considering your application																

Indicate any foreign languages you can speak, read and / or write			
	FLUENT	GOOD	FAIR
SPEAK			
READ			
WRITE			

List professional, trade, business or civic activities and offices held.
You may exclude memberships which would reveal sex, race, religion, national origin, age, ancestry, or handicap or other protected status:

_____

_____

_____

_____

References

Give name, address and telephone number of three references who are not related to you and are not previous employers.

1. _____

2. _____

3. _____

Have you ever had any job-related training in the United States military?

☐ Yes   ☐ No

If Yes, please describe _____

Are you physically or otherwise unable to perform the duties of the job for which you are applying?   ☐ Yes   ☐ No

Employment Experience

Start with your present or last job. Include any job-related military service assignments and volunteer activities. You may exclude organizations which indicate race, color, religion, gender, national origin, handicap or other protected status.

1. Employer	Dates Employed		**Work Performed**
	From	To	
Address			
Telephone Number(s)	Hourly Rate/Salary		
	Starting	Final	
Job Title	Supervisor		
Reason for Leaving			
2. Employer	Dates Employed		**Work Performed**
	From	To	
Address			
Telephone Number(s)	Hourly Rate/Salary		
	Starting	Final	
Job Title	Supervisor		
Reason for Leaving			
3. Employer	Dates Employed		**Work Performed**
	From	To	
Address			
Telephone Number(s)	Hourly Rate/Salary		
	Starting	Final	
Job Title	Supervisor		
Reason for Leaving			
4. Employer	Dates Employed		**Work Performed**
	From	To	
Address			
Telephone Number(s)	Hourly Rate/Salary		
	Starting	Final	
Job Title	Supervisor		
Reason for Leaving			

If you need additional space, please continue on a separate sheet of paper.

Special Skills and Qualifications

Summarize special job-related skills and qualifications acquired from employment or other experience.

Applicant's Statement

I certify that answers given herein are true and complete to the best of my knowledge.

I authorize investigation of all statements contained in this application for employment as may be necessary in arriving at an employment decision.

This application for employment shall be considered active for a period of time not to exceed 45 days. Any applicant wishing to be considered for employment beyond this time period should inquire as to whether or not applications are being accepted at that time.

I hereby understand and acknowledge that, unless otherwise defined by applicable law, any employment relationship with this organization is of an *"at will"* nature, which means that the Employee may resign at any time and the Employer may discharge Employee at any time with or without cause. It is further understood that this *"at will"* employment relationship may not be changed by any written document or by conduct unless such change is specifically acknowledged in writing by an authorized executive of this organization.

In the event of employment, I understand that false or misleading information given in my application or interview(s) may result in discharge. I understand, also, that I am required to abide by all rules and regulations of the employer.

Signature of Applicant	Date

FOR PERSONNEL DEPARTMENT USE ONLY

Arrange Interview ☐ Yes ☐ No

Remarks _____

_____
INTERVIEWER   DATE

Employed ☐ Yes ☐ No   Date of Employment _____

Job Title _____   Hourly Rate/ Salary _____ Department_____

By _____
NAME AND TITLE   DATE

NOTES _____

_____

_____

_____

Appendix A

Nationally Recognized
Accrediting Agencies and Associations

The following regional and national accrediting agencies and associations were recognized by the U.S. Secretary of Education in 1990 as reliable authorities on the quality of secondary, postsecondary education or training offered by educational institutions or programs. Contact any of the appropriate agencies or associations to check whether the educational institution or training program you're considering is accredited and approved.

REGIONAL INSTITUTIONAL ACCREDITING ASSOCIATIONS AND COMMISSIONS FOR HIGH SCHOOLS, COMMUNITY COLLEGES, JUNIOR COLLEGES, TECHNICAL INSTITUTES AND FOUR-YEAR COLLEGES AND UNIVERSITIES

Middle States Association of Colleges and Schools (Delaware, District of Columbia, Maryland, New Jersey, New York, Pennsylvania, Puerto Rico, Virgin Islands), 3624 Market Street, Philadelphia, PA 19104. Tel. (215) 662-5606.

New England Association of Schools and Colleges (Connecticut, Maine, Massachusetts, New Hampshire, Rhode Island, Vermont), Sanborn House, 15 High Street, Winchester, MA 01890. Tel. (617) 729-6762

North Central Association of Colleges and Schools (Arizona, Arkansas, Colorado, Illinois, Indiana, Iowa, Kansas, Michigan, Minnesota, Missouri, Nebraska, New Mexico, North Dakota, Ohio, Oklahoma, South Dakota, West Virginia, Wisconsin, Wyoming), 159 North Dearborn Street, Chicago, Illinois 60601. Tel. (800) 621-7440.

Northwest Association of Schools and Colleges (Alaska, Idaho, Montana, Nevada, Oregon, Utah, Washington), 3700-B University Way, NE, Seattle, WA 98105. Tel. (206) 543-0195.

Southern Association of Colleges and Schools (Alabama, Florida, Georgia, Kentucky, Louisiana, Mississippi, North Carolina, South Carolina,

131

Tennessee, Texas, Virginia), 1866 Southern Lane, Decatur, GA 30033-4097. Tel. (800) 248-7701.

Western Association of Schools and Colleges (California, Hawaii), 9053 Soquel Drive, Aptos, CA 95003. Tel. (408) 688-7575.

PROPRIETARY (PRIVATE) TRADE AND TECHNICAL
SCHOOLS

National Association of Trade and Technical Schools, P.O. Box 10429, Rockville MD 10850.

SPECIALIZED ACCREDITING ASSOCIATIONS AND AGENCIES

Art
National Association of Schools of Art and Design, 11250 Roger Bacon Drive, No. 5, Reston, VA 22090. Tel. (703) 437-0700.

Blind and visually handicapped education
National Accreditation Council for Agencies Serving the Blind and Visually Handicapped, 232 Madison Avenue, Suite 907, New York, NY. Tel. (212) 779-8080.

Business
Accrediting Commission, Association of Independent Schools and Colleges, One Dupont Circle, NW, Washington, DC 20036. Tel. (202) 659-2460.

Computer science
Computer Science Accreditation Commission, 345 East 47th Street, New York, NY 10017. Tel. (212) 705-7314.

Construction education
American Council for Construction Education, 1015 15th Street, NW, Washington, DC 20005. Tel. (202) 347-5875.

Continuing (adult) education
Accrediting Council for Continuing Education and Training, 530 East Main Street, Richmond, VA 23219. Tel. (804) 648-6742.

Cosmetology
National Accrediting Commission of Cosmetology Arts and Sciences, 1333 H Street, NW, Washington, DC 20005. Tel. (202) 289-4300.

Dance
Commission on Accreditation, National Association of Schools of Dance, 11250 Roger Bacon Drive, No. 5, Reston, VA 22090. Tel. (703) 437-0700.

Dental technology
Commission of Dental Accreditation, American Dental Association, 211 East Chicago Avenue, Chicago, IL 60611. Tel. (312) 440-2500.

Funeral service education
Committee on Accreditation, American Board of Funeral Service Education, 23 Crestwood Road, Cumberland, ME 04201. Tel. (207) 829-5715.

Health services administration
Accrediting Bureau of Health Education Schools, Oak Manor Offices, 29089 U.S. 20 West, Elkhart, IN 46514, (219) 293-0124 and Committee on Allied Health Education and Accreditation, American Medical Association, 535 North Dearborn Street, Chicago, IL 60610, (312) 645-4660 for all training to become a blood bank technologist, cytotechnologist, diagnostic medical sonographer, electroencephalographic technologist, emergency medical technician-paramedic, histologic technician/technologist, medical assistant, medical laboratory technician (certificate and associate degree), medical record administrator and medical record technician, medical technologist, nuclear medicine technologist, occupational therapist, ophthalmic medical assistant, perfusionist, radiation therapy technologist and radiographer, respiratory therapist and respiratory therapy technician, surgical technologist.

Home study education
National Home Study Council, 1601 18th Street, NW, Washington, DC 20009. Tel. (202) 234-5100.

Interior design
Foundation for Interior Design Education Research, 60 Monroe Center, NW., Grand Rapids, MI 49503. Tel. (616) 458-0400.

Music
National Association of Schools of Music, 11250 Roger Bacon Drive, No. 5, Reston, VA 22090. Tel. (703) 437-0700.

Nursing
American Association of Nurse Anesthetists, 216 Higgins Road, Park Ridge, IL 60068. Tel. (312) 692-7050.

American College of Nurse-Midwives, 1522 K Street NW, Washington, DC 20005. Tel. (202) 347-5445.

National League for Nursing, 10 Columbus Circle, New York, NY 10019. Tel. (212) 582-1022.

Opticianry
Commission on Opticianry Accreditation, 10111 Martin Luther King Jr. Highway, Suite 110, Bowie, MD. Tel. (301) 577-4829.

Optometry
American Optometric Association, 243 North Lindbergh Blvd., St. Louis, MO 63141. Tel. (314) 991-4100.

Physical therapy
American Physical Therapy Association, Trans Potomac Plaza, 1111 North Fairfax Street, Alexandria, VA 22314. Tel. (703) 684-2782.

Rehabilitation training
Commission on Accreditation of Rehabilitation Facilities, 2500 North Pantano Road, Tucson, AZ 85715. Tel. (602) 886-8575.

Theater
National Association of Schools of Theater, 11250 Roger Bacon Drive, No. 5, Reston, VA 22090. Tel. (703) 437-0700.

Veterinary medicine
American Veterinary Medical Association, 930 North Meacham Road, Schaumburg, IL 60196. Tel. (312) 885-8070.

National Apprenticeship Program

U.S. DEPARTMENT OF LABOR
EMPLOYMENT AND TRAINING ADMINISTRATION

State Offices
Bureau of Apprenticeship and Training
(To Check On Accreditation of Apprenticeship Programs)

ALABAMA
2017 2ND AVE., N.
BIRMINGHAM   35205

ALASKA
ROOM C-528
701 C STREET
ANCHORAGE   99513

ARIZONA
SUITE 302
3221 N. 16TH STREET
PHOENIX   85016

ARKANSAS
ROOM 3014
700 W. CAPITOL
    STREET
LITTLE ROCK   72201

CALIFORNIA
ROOM 350
211 MAIN STREET
SAN FRANCISCO   94105

COLORADO
ROOM 480
721 19TH STREET
DENVER   80202

CONNECTICUT
ROOM 367
135 HIGH STREET
HARTFORD   06103

DELAWARE
FEDERAL BUILDING
844 KING STREET
WILMINGTON   19801

FLORIDA
ROOM 1049
227 N. BRONOUGH
    STREET
TALLAHASSEE   32301

GEORGIA
ROOM 418
1371 PEACHTREET ST.,
    NE
ATLANTA   30367

HAWAII
ROOM 5113
300 ALA MOANA BLVD.
HONOLULU   96850

IDAHO
ROOM 493
550 W. FORT STREET
BOISE   83724

ILLINOIS
ROOM 702
230 S. DEARBORN
    STREET
CHICAGO   60604

INDIANA
ROOM 414
46 E. OHIO STREET
INDIANAPOLIS   46204

IOWA
ROOM 637
210 WALNUT STREET
DES MOINES   50309

KANSAS
ROOM 235
444 SE QUINCY ST.
TOPEKA   66683

KENTUCKY
ROOM 554-C
600 FEDERAL PLACE
LOUISVILLE   40202

LOUISIANA
ROOM 925
600 S. MAESTRI ST.
NEW ORLEANS   70130

MAINE
ROOM 101-B
68 SEWALL STREET
AUGUSTA   04330

MARYLAND
ROOM 1028
31 HOPKINS PLAZA
BALTIMORE   21201

MASSACHUSETTS
ROOM 510-B
JFK FED. BLDG.
BOSTON   02203

MICHIGAN
ROOM 657
231 W. LAFAYETTE
   AVE.
DETROIT   48226

MINNESOTA
ROOM 134
316 ROBERT ST.
ST. PAUL   55101

MISSISSIPPI
SUITE 1010
100 W. CAPITOL ST.
JACKSON   39269

MISSOURI
ROOM 547
210 N. TUCKER
ST. LOUIS   63101

MONTANA
ROOM 394
301 S. PARK AVE.
HELENA   59626-0055

NEBRASKA
ROOM 700
106 S. 15TH ST.
OMAHA   68102

NEVADA
ROOM 311
301 E. STEWART AVE.
LAS VEGAS   89101

NEW HAMPSHIRE
ROOM 311
55 PLEASANT ST.
CONCORD   03301

NEW JERSEY
ROOM 339
60 PARK PLACE
NEWARK   07102

NEW MEXICO
SUITE 16
320 CENTRAL AVE.,
   SW
ALBUQUERQUE   87102

NEW YORK
ROOM 810
FEDERAL BLDG.
ALBANY   12207

NORTH CAROLINA
ROOM 376
310 NEW BERN AVE.
RALEIGH   27601

NORTH DAKOTA
ROOM 344
653 2ND AVE., N.
FARGO   58102

OHIO
ROOM 605
200 N. HIGH ST.
COLUMBUS   43215

OKLAHOMA
ROOM 526
200 NW FIFTH ST.
OKLAHOMA
   CITY   73102

OREGON
ROOM 526
1220 SW 3RD AVE.
PORTLAND   97204

PENNSYLVANIA
ROOM 773
228 WALNUT STREET
HARRISBURG   17108

RHODE ISLAND
100 HARTFORD AVE.
PROVIDENCE   02909

SOUTH CAROLINA
ROOM 838
1835 ASSEMBLY ST.
COLUMBIA   29201

SOUTH DAKOTA
ROOM 403
300 N. DAKOTA AVE.
SIOUX FALLS   57102

TENNESSEE
SUITE 101-A
460 METROPLEX DR.
NASHVILLE   37211

TEXAS
ROOM 2102
2320 LABRANCH ST.
HOUSTON   77004

UTAH
ROOM 1051
1745 W. 1700 SOUTH
SALT LAKE
   CITY   84104

VERMONT
SUITE 103
96 COLLEGE ST.
BURLINGTON   05401

VIRGINIA
ROOM 10-020
400 N. 8TH ST.
RICHMOND   23240

WASHINGTON
ROOM B-104
909 FIRST AVE.
SEATTLE   98174

WEST VIRGINIA
ROOM 310
550 EAGAN ST.
CHARLESTON   25301

WISCONSIN
ROOM 303
212 E. WASH. AVE.
MADISON   53703

WYOMING
ROOM 8017
2120 CAPITOL AVE.
CHEYENNE   82001

Appendix B

Essential Employability Skills

Together with employers, community leaders and educators, the Colorado Department of Education developed the following list of "employability skills" that every good career education program should be teaching its students. If your school's vocational education program is not teaching most of these skills, it is not preparing you for the world of work. If you cannot find a high school career education program that teaches these skills, switch to a strong academic program and postpone plans for vocational education until you graduate from high school and can enroll in a community college, technical institute or some other post-high school career training program.

Identification of Essential Employability Skills

DIRECTIONS: Check those skills that are essential for students to acquire so that they will be well prepared to obtain employment and be successful on the job. In making judgments consider your own job experience. Add to part "M. Other" any skills which you consider essential which are not listed.

Name _____

Date _____

Please refer to the handout entitled "Identification of Employability Skills" for examples of each skill.

A. JOB SEEKING—CAREER DEVELOPMENT SKILLS
- ☐ 1. Knows sources of information
- ☐ 2. Knows own abilities, aptitudes, interests
- ☐ 3. Knows occupational characteristics
- ☐ ·4. Identifies career/occupational goals
- ☐ 5. Develops a career plan
- ☐ 6. Identifies and researches potential employers
- ☐ 7. Knows employment position(s) desired
- ☐ 8. Accurately completes:
- ☐   a. Inquiry letter
- ☐   b. Resume
- ☐   c. Follow-up letter
- ☐ 9. Accurately completes job application
- ☐ 10. Handles interview without errors
- ☐ 11. Seeks information about future education/training

B. MATH SKILLS
- ☐ 1. Understands importance of math in jobs
- ☐ 2. Performs basic calculations (+, −, ×, ÷)
- ☐ 3. Performs calculations in:
- ☐   a. Fractions
- ☐   b. Percentages
- ☐   c. Proportions/Ratios
- ☐ 4. Makes reasonable estimates
- ☐ 5. Uses values from graphs, maps, tables
- ☐ 6. Uses English/metric measurement

- ☐ 7. Compares numerical values
- ☐ 8. Applies geometric principles
- ☐ 9. Uses formulas correctly
- ☐ 10. Constructs diagrams, tables, records
- ☐ 11. Uses elementary statistics
- ☐ 12. Uses instruments to solve problems:
- ☐   a. Gauges, Meters, Scales
- ☐   b. Calculators
- ☐   c. Computers

C. COMPUTER SKILLS
- ☐ 1. Becomes aware of computer functions
- ☐ 2. Inputs and accesses data from computer
- ☐ 3. Has experience with computer programs
- ☐   a. Business applications
- ☐   b. Data management
- ☐   c. Simple programming
- ☐   d. Word processing
- ☐ 4. Understands issues associated with computer use

D. READING SKILLS
- ☐ 1. Understands the importance of reading in jobs
- ☐ 2. Develops vocabulary related to careers and occupations
- ☐ 3. Reads for details and special information
- ☐ 4. Interprets pictures, graphs, and symbols
- ☐ 5. Locates information in reference materials
- ☐ 6. Follows intent of written directions/instructions
- ☐ 7. Interprets ideas and concepts (comprehension)
- ☐ 8. Reads accurately at appropriate rate

E. WRITING SKILLS
- ☐ 1. Understands the importance of writing in jobs
- ☐ 2. Develops handwriting legibility
- ☐ 3. Composes formal letters
- ☐ 4. Fills out forms
- ☐ 5. Records messages
- ☐ 6. Writes memorandums
- ☐ 7. Composes ads/telegrams
- ☐ 8. Writes instructions and directions
- ☐ 9. Writes reports
- ☐ 10. Develops summaries
- ☐ 11. Takes notes and/or outlines
- ☐ 12. Corrects written materials

F. COMMUNICATION SKILLS
- ☐ 1. Reports accurately/concisely
- ☐ 2. Follows intent of oral directions/instructions
- ☐ 3. Speaks distinctly
- ☐ 4. Formulates questions
- ☐ 5. Answers questions accurately
- ☐ 6. Explains activities and ideas clearly
- ☐ 7. Uses appropriate vocabulary/grammar
- ☐ 8. Gives clear instructions and directions
- ☐ 9. Stays on topic
- ☐ 10. Uses nonverbal signs appropriately
- ☐ 11. Develops oral presentations
- ☐ 12. Presents information effectively to groups

G. INTERPERSONAL SKILLS
- ☐ 1. Functions cooperatively with fellow students
- ☐ 2. Functions cooperatively in team efforts
- ☐ 3. Functions cooperatively with adults outside school
- ☐ 4. Exhibits openness and flexibility
- ☐ 5. Seeks clarification of instructions
- ☐ 6. Exercises patience and tolerance
- ☐ 7. Utilizes suggestions about improving skills
- ☐ 8. Uses initiative in getting work done
- ☐ 9. Expresses opinions with tact
- ☐ 10. Demonstrates ability to negotiate differences with others

H. BUSINESS ECONOMIC SKILLS
- ☐ 1. Understands business organization
- ☐ 2. Understands business competition
- ☐ 3. Knows about processes of marketing
- ☐ 4. Knows about processes of production
- ☐ 5. Understands business costs
- ☐ 6. Understands factors affecting profits

I. PERSONAL ECONOMIC SKILLS
- ☐ 1. Knows how to evaluate products and services
- ☐ 2. Knows how to access community resources/services
- ☐ 3. Can compute working hours/wages
- ☐ 4. Knows how to handle financial affairs
- ☐ 5. Can handle records of income and expenses
- ☐ 6. Knows how to make price-quality comparisons
- ☐ 7. Knows how to prepare state/federal tax forms
- ☐ 8. Can evaluate insurance programs
- ☐ 9. Knows how to determine credit costs
- ☐ 10. Understands legal rights in agreements
- ☐ 11. Maintains and utilizes various forms of transportation

J. MANUAL PERCEPTUAL SKILLS
- ☐ 1. Constructs/assembles materials
- ☐ 2. Uses specific hand tools and instruments
- ☐ 3. Develops visual presentations
- ☐ 4. Masters keyboard skills
- ☐ 5. Operates power equipment

K. WORK ACTIVITY SKILLS
- ☐ 1. Produces type/amount of work required
- ☐ 2. Maintains punctuality
- ☐ 3. Meets attendance requirements
- ☐ 4. Accepts assignments/responsibilities
- ☐ 5. Takes responsibility for own actions
- ☐ 6. Maintains consistent effort
- ☐ 7. Works independently
- ☐ 8. Manages time effectively

☐ 9. Respects rights and property of others
☐ 10. Adheres to policies and regulations
☐ a. Health
☐ b. Honesty
☐ c. Safety
☐ 11. Presents a neat appearance
☐ 12. Keeps work area in good/safe condition
☐ 13. Exhibits interest in future career
☐ 14. Suggests or makes workplace improvements
☐ 15. Knows sources of continuing education
☐ 16. Knows about basic employee/ student rights
☐ 17. Knows about basic employee/ student responsibilities
☐ 18. Knows basic steps in getting a raise or promotion
☐ 19. Knows how to terminate employment

L. PROBLEM SOLVING/REASONING SKILLS
☐ 1. Recognizes problems that need solution

☐ 2. Identifies procedures
☐ 3. Obtains resources
☐ 4. Prepares or sets up materials/ equipment
☐ 5. Collects information
☐ 6. Organizes information
☐ 7. Interprets information
☐ 8. Formulates alternative approaches
☐ 9. Selects efficient approaches
☐ 10. Reviews progress
☐ 11. Evaluates activities
☐ 12. Corrects errors
☐ 13. Makes conclusions
☐ 14. Summarizes and communicates results
☐ 15. Uses results to develop new ideas

M. OTHER
☐ 1. _____
☐ 2. _____
☐ 3. _____
☐ 4. _____
☐ 5. _____
☐ 6. _____
☐ 7. _____
☐ 8. _____
☐ 9. _____

Source: Colorado Department of Education

Appendix C

Median Weekly Pay
In 600 Different Jobs

Here are the median weekly earnings in 1989 of salaried workers in a wide variety of different jobs, ranging from doctors to bartenders and requiring vast differences in training and formal education. As you'll see, there are significant differences in the salaries paid to men and women, with women receiving far less on average. The figures are compiled annually by the U.S. Department of Labor's Bureau of Labor Statistics.

MEDIAN WEEKLY EARNINGS OF WAGE AND SALARY WORKERS WHO USUALLY WORK FULL TIME, BY DETAILED OCCUPATION AND SEX, 1989 ANNUAL AVERAGES

(Numbers in thousands)

Occupation	Both sexes		Men		Women		Women's earnings as a percent of men's	Women as a Percent of total employed
	Number of workers	Median weekly earnings	Number of workers	Median weekly earnings	Number of workers	Median weekly earnings		
Total	84,553	$399	48,949	$468	35,605	$328	70.1	42.1
Managerial and professional specialty occupations	22,645	583	12,281	693	10,363	488	70.4	45.8
Executive, administrative, and managerial occupations	11,335	579	6,544	698	4,791	458	65.6	42.3
Legislators, chief execs., and genl admstrs., pub. adm.	29	—	22	—	7	—	—	—
Administrators and officials, public administration	484	585	280	650	204	504	77.5	42.1
Administrators, protective service	58	570	50	623	9	—	—	15.5
Financial managers	441	667	252	848	189	510	60.1	42.9
Personnel and labor relations managers	126	668	59	909	66	520	57.2	52.4
Purchasing managers	111	651	86	772	26	—	—	23.4
Managers, marketing, advertising and public relations	495	753	346	862	150	540	62.6	30.3
Administrators, education and related fields	495	712	262	818	233	573	70.0	47.1
Managers, medicine and health	178	604	56	734	122	556	75.7	68.5
Managers, properties and real estate	259	424	127	500	131	368	73.6	50.6
Postmasters and mail superintendents	29	—	19	—	10	—	—	—
Funeral directors	21	—	19	—	2	—	—	—
Managers and administrators, n.e.c.	5,283	589	3,370	714	1,913	421	59.0	36.2
Management-related occupations	3,326	516	1,597	615	1,729	453	73.7	52.0
Accountants and auditors	1,187	522	591	620	596	463	74.7	50.2
Underwriters and other financial officers	715	543	351	684	364	465	68.0	50.9
Management analysts	88	693	54	761	34	—	—	38.6
Personnel, training and labor relations specialists	387	553	156	645	231	491	76.1	59.7
Purchasing agents and buyers, farm products	5	—	4	—	0	—	—	—

Buyers, wholesale and retail trade, exc. farm pdts.	153	475	82	542	72	376	69.4	47.1
Purchasing agents and buyers, n.e.c.	240	512	131	580	109	412	71.0	45.4
Business and promotion agents	10	—	6	—	4	—	—	—
Construction inspectors	55	536	53	542	3	481	91.8	5.5
Inspectors and compliance officers, exc. construction	169	511	118	524	50	417	77.9	29.6
Management-related occupations, n.e.c.	317	436	51	535	267	—	—	84.2
Professional specialty occupations	11,310	586	5,737	688	5,572	506	73.5	49.3
Engineers, architects, and surveyors	1,797	771	1,639	782	158	630	80.6	8.8
Architects	107	667	83	756	24	—	—	22.4
Engineers	1,667	775	1,534	784	133	672	85.7	8.0
Aerospace engineers	110	801	106	805	3	—	—	2.7
Metallurgical and materials engineers	19	—	18	—	1	—	—	—
Mining engineers	4	—	2	—	1	—	—	—
Petroleum engineers	19	807	17	821	2	—	—	15.5
Chemical engineers	58	—	50	—	9	—	—	—
Nuclear engineers	10	—	10	—	0	—	—	—
Civil engineers	230	735	218	742	11	—	—	4.8
Agricultural engineers	2	—	2	—	0	—	—	—
Electrical and electronic engineers	512	803	467	808	45	—	—	8.8
Industrial engineers	190	710	167	732	23	—	—	12.1
Mechanical engineers	289	766	273	774	16	—	—	5.5
Marine engineers and naval architects	14	—	14	—	0	—	—	—
Engineers, n.e.c.	211	761	189	771	21	—	—	10.0
Surveyors and mapping scientists	22	—	22	—	0	—	—	—
Mathematical and computer scientists	767	695	501	738	267	604	81.8	34.8
Computer systems analysts and scientists	497	711	342	747	155	620	83.0	31.2
Operations and systems researchers and analysts	225	662	133	710	92	594	83.7	40.9
Actuaries	16	—	8	—	8	—	—	—
Statisticians	22	—	11	—	10	—	—	—
Mathematical scientists, n.e.c.	8	—	6	—	2	—	—	—

145

MEDIAN WEEKLY EARNINGS OF WAGE AND SALARY WORKERS WHO USUALLY WORK FULL TIME, BY DETAILED OCCUPATION AND SEX, 1989 ANNUAL AVERAGES

(Numbers in thousands)

Occupation	Both sexes		Men		Women		Women's earnings as a percent of men's	Women as a Percent of total employed
	Number of workers	Median weekly earnings	Number of workers	Median weekly earnings	Number of workers	Median weekly earnings		
Natural scientists	346	642	253	699	93	544	77.8	26.9
Physicists and astronomers	24	—	23	—	1	—	—	—
Chemists, except biochemists	107	633	78	700	29	—	—	27.1
Atmospheric and space scientists	6	—	4	—	2	—	—	—
Geologists and geodesists	42	—	34	—	8	—	—	—
Physical scientists, n.e.c.	19	—	14	—	5	—	—	—
Agricultural and food scientists	15	—	8	—	7	—	—	—
Biological and life scientists	64	572	43	—	21	—	—	32.8
Forestry and conservation scientists	29	—	24	—	4	—	—	—
Medical scientists	41	—	25	—	16	—	—	—
Health diagnosing occupations	288	786	216	871	72	600	68.9	25.0
Physicians	242	792	181	887	60	623	70.2	24.8
Dentists	17	—	17	—	0	—	—	—
Veterinarians	15	—	9	—	5	—	—	—
Optometrists	6	—	3	—	3	—	—	—
Podiatrists	1	—	0	—	1	—	—	—
Health diagnosing practitioners, n.e.c.	8	—	6	—	2	—	—	—
Health assessment and treating occupations	1,577	564	266	634	1,311	551	86.9	83.1
Registered nurses	1,113	569	79	629	1,035	564	89.7	93.0
Pharmacists	114	748	75	768	38	—	—	33.3
Dietitians	59	428	4	—	55	428	—	93.2

146

Therapists	230	511	64	565	167	496	87.8	72.6
Inhalation therapists	47	—	26	—	21	—	—	—
Occupational therapists	28	—	0	—	28	—	—	76.4
Physical therapists	55	534	13	—	42	—	—	—
Speech therapists	48	—	6	—	42	—	—	65.4
Therapists, n.e.c.	52	457	19	—	34	—	—	26.7
Physicians' assistants	60	513	44	—	16	—	—	—
Teachers, college and university	493	711	342	785	152	581	74.0	30.8
Earth, environmental and marine science teachers	4	—	3	—	1	—	—	—
Biological science teachers	13	—	8	—	5	—	—	—
Chemistry teachers	10	—	9	—	1	—	—	—
Physics teachers	8	—	7	—	1	—	—	—
Natural science teachers, n.e.c.	1	—	1	—	0	—	—	—
Psychology teachers	12	—	10	—	2	—	—	—
Economics teachers	15	—	13	—	2	—	—	—
History teachers	8	—	8	—	0	—	—	—
Political science teachers	7	—	7	—	1	—	—	—
Sociology teachers	5	—	5	—	1	—	—	—
Social science teachers, n.e.c.	3	—	3	—	1	—	—	—
Engineering teachers	20	—	20	—	0	—	—	—
Mathematical science teachers	37	—	32	—	5	—	—	—
Computer science teachers	14	—	9	—	5	—	—	—
Medical science teachers	8	—	5	—	3	—	—	—
Health specialties teachers	24	—	8	—	16	—	—	—
Business, commerce and marketing teachers	22	—	16	—	6	—	—	—
Agriculture and forestry teachers	5	—	5	—	0	—	—	—
Art, drama and music teachers	31	—	19	—	12	—	—	—
Physical education teachers	8	—	4	—	4	—	—	—
Education teachers	9	—	6	—	3	—	—	—
English teachers	37	—	17	—	20	—	—	—
Foreign language teachers	13	—	6	—	7	—	—	—
Law teachers	7	—	5	—	2	—	—	—

MEDIAN WEEKLY EARNINGS OF WAGE AND SALARY WORKERS WHO USUALLY WORK FULL TIME, BY DETAILED OCCUPATION AND SEX, 1989 ANNUAL AVERAGES

(Numbers in thousands)

Occupation	Both sexes		Men		Women		Women's earnings as a percent of men's	Women as a Percent of total employed
	Number of workers	Median weekly earnings	Number of workers	Median weekly earnings	Number of workers	Median weekly earnings		
Social work teachers	0	—	0	—	0	—	—	—
Theology teachers	12	—	10	—	1	—	—	—
Trade and industrial teacheres	3	—	1	—	2	—	—	—
Home economics teachers	2	—	0	—	2	—	—	—
Teachers, postsecondary, n.e.c.	6	—	6	—	0	—	—	—
Postsecondary teachers, subject not specified	147	676	97	775	50	542	69.9	34.0
Teachers, except college and university	3,148	503	926	568	2,222	486	85.6	70.6
Teachers, prekindergarten and kindergarten	275	373	9	—	265	374	—	96.4
Teachers, elementary school	1,315	498	214	544	1,102	491	90.3	83.8
Teachers, secondary school	1,082	545	544	579	538	517	89.3	49.7
Teachers, special education	241	500	36	—	205	490	—	85.1
Teachers, n.e.c.	235	464	123	523	112	408	78.0	47.7
Counselors, educational and vocational	177	598	79	650	97	553	85.1	54.8
Librarians, archivists and curators	147	483	26	—	121	477	—	82.3
Librarians	133	483	19	—	113	479	—	85.0
Archivists and curators	14	—	7	—	7	—	—	—
Social scientists and urban planners	253	609	141	708	113	522	73.7	44.7
Economists	115	704	68	809	46	—	—	40.0
Psychologists	106	523	51	603	55	501	83.1	51.9
Sociologists	3	—	2	—	1	—	—	—

Occupation								
Social scientists, n.e.c.	12	—	7	—	4	—	—	—
Urban planners	17	—	12	—	5	—	—	—
Social, recreation and religious workers	844	411	448	434	396	392	90.3	46.9
Social workers	455	438	151	491	304	418	85.1	66.8
Recreation workers	75	261	23	—	52	253	—	69.3
Clergy	270	410	256	419	14	—	—	5.2
Religious workers, n.e.c.	44	—	19	—	25	—	—	—
Lawyers and judges	424	993	301	1,021	123	733	71.8	29.0
Lawyers	391	990	276	1,016	115	749	73.7	29.4
Judges	33	—	25	—	8	—	—	—
Writers, artists, entertainers and athletes	1,050	488	600	559	450	413	73.9	42.9
Authors	10	—	4	—	6	—	—	—
Technical writers	58	623	32	595	27	—	—	46.6
Designers	321	489	194	—	127	345	58.0	39.6
Musicians and composers	30	—	22	—	7	—	—	—
Actors and directors	52	494	33	—	19	—	—	36.5
Painters, sculptors, craft artists and artist printmakers	99	427	52	485	47	—	—	47.5
Photographers	53	349	34	—	19	—	—	35.8
Dancers	5	—	0	—	5	—	—	—
Artists, performers and related workers, n.e.c.	26	—	14	—	12	—	—	—
Editors and reporters	205	494	112	589	93	442	75.0	45.4
Public relations specialists	125	576	46	—	79	493	—	63.2
Announcers	29	—	25	—	4	—	—	—
Athletes	37	—	31	—	5	—	—	—
Technical, sales and administrative support occupations	25,195	359	9,332	480	15,863	317	66.0	63.0
Technicians and related support occupations	3,042	475	1,666	538	1,376	403	74.9	45.2
Health technologists and technicians	972	380	203	467	769	367	78.6	79.1
Clinical laboratory technologists and technicians	250	423	70	478	179	412	86.2	71.6
Dental hygienists	33	—	0	—	33	—	—	—

MEDIAN WEEKLY EARNINGS OF WAGE AND SALARY WORKERS WHO USUALLY WORK FULL TIME, BY DETAILED OCCUPATION AND SEX, 1989 ANNUAL AVERAGES

(Numbers in thousands)

Occupation	Both sexes		Men		Women		Women's earnings as a percent of men's	Women as a Percent of total employed
	Number of workers	Median weekly earnings	Number of workers	Median weekly earnings	Number of workers	Median weekly earnings		
Health record technologists and technicians	63	307	7	—	56	316	—	88.9
Radiologic technicians	99	435	31	—	68	410	—	68.7
Licensed practical nurses	306	354	11	—	295	353	—	96.4
Health technologists and technicians, n.e.c.	222	351	84	464	137	322	69.4	61.7
Engineering and related technologists and technicians	848	492	686	506	162	428	84.6	19.1
Electrical and electronic technicians	295	512	249	521	46	—	—	15.6
Industrial engineering technicians	4	—	2	—	2	—	—	—
Mechanical engineering technicians	12	—	9	—	3	—	—	—
Engineering technicians, n.e.c.	205	480	154	503	50	363	72.2	24.4
Drafting occupations	272	486	217	499	54	446	89.4	19.9
Surveying and mapping technicians	61	436	55	423	6	—	—	9.8
Science technicians	178	476	134	500	44	—	—	24.7
Biological technicians	47	—	33	—	14	—	—	—
Chemical technicians	68	530	54	551	14	—	—	20.6
Science technicians, n.e.c.	62	486	48	—	15	—	—	—
Technicians, except health, engineering and science	1,044	578	642	633	401	492	77.7	38.4
Airplane pilots and navigators	77	807	76	809	1	—	—	1.3
Air traffic controllers	33	—	27	—	6	—	—	—
Broadcast equipment operators	22	—	14	—	8	—	—	—

Occupation							
Computer programmers	511	606	328	651	182	541	83.1	35.6
Tool programmers, numerical control	4	—	4	—	0	—	—	78.6
Legal assistants	173	469	37	—	136	460	—	30.5
Technicians, n.e.c.	223	498	155	524	68	415	79.2	
Sales occupations	7,982	384	4,581	487	3,401	278	57.1	42.6
Supervisors and proprietors	2,354	424	1,507	495	846	329	66.5	35.9
Sales representatives, finance and business services	1,493	502	812	612	681	408	66.7	45.6
Insurance sales	333	513	206	603	127	422	70.0	38.1
Real estate sales	351	505	162	675	189	432	64.0	53.8
Securities and financial service sales	238	651	162	773	75	484	62.6	31.5
Advertising and related sales	120	428	54	480	66	409	85.2	55.0
Sales occupations, other business services	451	455	228	569	223	364	64.0	49.4
Sales reps, commodities, exc. retail, inc. sales engrs.	1,306	561	1,055	582	251	492	84.5	19.2
Sales workers, retail and personal services	2,817	235	1,203	304	1,614	208	68.4	57.3
Sales workers, motor vehicles and boats	253	408	242	412	11	—	—	4.3
Sales workers, apparel	150	220	31	—	118	208	—	78.7
Sales workers, shoes	41	—	21	410	20	—	—	
Sales workers, furniture and home furnishings	88	360	50	344	38	—	—	43.2
Sales workers, radio, tv, hi-fi and appliances	137	321	108	313	29	—	—	21.2
Sales workers, hardware and building supplies	147	289	116	293	31	—	—	21.1
Sales workers, parts	139	287	133	280	6	—	—	4.3
Sales workers, other commodities	632	229	209	—	423	215	76.8	66.9
Sales counter clerks	95	214	27	—	67	196	—	70.5
Cashiers	1,042	202	224	211	818	200	94.8	78.5
Street and door-to-door sales workers	86	320	35	—	51	294	—	59.3
News vendors	8	—	7	—	1	—	—	—
Sales-related occupations	13	—	4	—	9	—	—	—
Demonstrators, promoters, and models, sales	5	—	1	—	3	—	—	—
Auctioneers	1	—	1	—	0	—	—	—
Sales support occupations, n.e.c.	7	—	2	—	6	—	—	—

MEDIAN WEEKLY EARNINGS OF WAGE AND SALARY WORKERS WHO USUALLY WORK FULL TIME, BY DETAILED OCCUPATION AND SEX, 1989 ANNUAL AVERAGES

(Numbers in thousands)

Occupation	Both sexes		Men		Women		Women's earnings as a percent of men's	Women as a Percent of total employed
	Number of workers	Median weekly earnings	Number of workers	Median weekly earnings	Number of workers	Median weekly earnings		
Administrative support occupations, including clerical	14,171	331	3,085	421	11,085	316	75.1	78.2
Supervisors, administrative support	731	490	306	599	425	427	71.3	58.1
Supervisors, general office	438	465	150	615	288	408	66.3	65.8
Supervisors, computer equipment operators	38	—	21	—	16	504	—	—
Supervisors, financial records processing	86	546	28	—	59	—	—	68.6
Chief communications operators	1	—	0	—	1	—	—	—
Supervisors, distribution, scheduling and adjusting clerks	168	516	106	539	61	492	91.3	36.3
Computer equipment operators	760	356	283	417	477	320	76.7	62.8
Computer operators	753	357	282	418	472	321	76.8	62.7
Peripheral equipment operators	7	—	1	—	5	—	—	—
Secretaries, stenographers and typists	3,659	325	49	—	3,610	325	—	98.7
Secretaries	3,141	328	29	—	3,113	327	—	99.1
Stenographers	25	—	3	—	22	—	—	—
Typists	493	311	18	—	475	311	—	96.3
Information clerks	981	277	107	340	874	274	80.6	89.1
Interviewers	144	336	22	—	122	327	—	84.7
Hotel clerks	68	231	19	—	49	—	—	72.1
Transportation ticket and reservation agents	101	392	33	—	67	373	—	66.3
Receptionists	522	261	11	—	510	260	—	97.7
Information clerks, n.e.c.	147	274	22	—	125	271	—	85.0

Records processing occupations, except financial	566	312	99	358	468	306	85.5	82.7
Classified-ad clerks	2	—	0	—	2	—	—	—
Correspondence clerks	17	—	2	—	15	—	—	—
Order clerks	165	380	29	—	136	365	—	82.4
Personnel clerks, except payroll and timekeeping	75	312	6	—	70	310	—	93.3
Library clerks	50	295	11	—	40	—	—	80.0
File clerks	172	275	38	—	133	268	—	77.3
Records clerks	85	331	13	—	72	324	—	84.7
Financial records processing occupations	1,604	317	153	392	1,451	313	79.8	90.5
Bookkeepers, accounting, and auditing clerks	1,219	318	105	376	1,114	315	83.8	91.4
Payroll and timekeeping clerks	147	326	14	—	133	318	—	90.5
Billing clerks	130	296	16	—	115	290	—	88.5
Cost and rate clerks	71	324	17	—	54	309	—	76.1
Billing, posting and calculating machine operators	36	—	1	—	35	—	—	—
Duplicating, mail and other office machine operators	46	—	15	—	32	—	—	—
Duplicating machine operators	18	—	7	—	11	—	—	—
Mail preparing and paper handling machine operators	9	—	2	—	8	—	—	—
Office machine operators, n.e.c.	19	—	6	—	13	—	—	—
Communications equipment operators	173	309	21	—	151	307	—	87.3
Telephone operators	165	308	18	—	147	306	—	89.1
Telegraphers	5	—	2	—	3	—	—	—
Communications equipment operators, n.e.c.	2	—	1	—	1	—	—	—
Mail and message distributing operators	783	493	530	511	253	451	88.3	32.3
Postal clerks, except mail carriers	287	509	173	523	113	492	94.1	39.4
Mail carriers, postal service	298	528	232	540	66	480	88.9	22.1
Mail clerks, except postal service	126	283	66	290	60	275	94.8	47.6
Messengers	72	308	58	322	14	—	—	19.4

MEDIAN WEEKLY EARNINGS OF WAGE AND SALARY WORKERS WHO USUALLY WORK FULL TIME, BY DETAILED OCCUPATION AND SEX, 1989 ANNUAL AVERAGES

(Numbers in thousands)

Occupation	Both sexes		Men		Women		Women's earnings as a percent of men's	Women as a Percent of total employed
	Number of workers	Median weekly earnings	Number of workers	Median weekly earnings	Number of workers	Median weekly earnings		
Material recording, scheduling and distr. clerks	1,478	343	906	371	571	310	83.6	38.6
Dispatchers	166	356	82	399	84	332	83.2	50.6
Production coordinators	203	439	116	490	87	387	79.0	42.9
Traffic, shipping, and receiving clerks	473	310	346	327	127	269	82.3	26.8
Stock and inventory clerks	443	331	267	358	176	305	85.2	39.7
Meter readers	45	—	36	—	9	—	—	—
Weighers, measurers and checkers	57	383	28	—	28	—	—	49.1
Samplers	1	—	0	—	1	—	—	—
Expediters	73	318	25	—	48	—	—	65.8
Material rec'dg. scheduling and distr. clerks, nec.	18	—	5	—	12	—	—	—
Adjusters and investigators	976	357	244	464	732	339	73.1	75.0
Insurance adjusters, examiners and investigators	302	381	80	491	222	353	71.9	73.5
Investigators and adjusters, except insurance	491	348	116	487	375	329	67.6	76.4
Eligibility clerks, social welfare	60	388	9	—	51	381	—	85.0
Bill and account collectors	124	334	39	—	84	330	—	67.7
Miscellaneous administrative support occupations	2,413	303	371	368	2,042	297	80.7	84.6
General office clerks	564	311	117	335	446	307	91.6	79.1
Bank tellers	370	264	30	—	341	263	—	92.2
Proofreaders	23	—	6	—	17	—	—	—
Data-entry keyers	361	303	38	—	323	300	—	89.5

154

Statistical clerks	80.0	—	384	56	—	13	394	70
Teachers' aides	97.3	—	234	219	—	6	234	225
Administrative support occupations, n.e.c.	79.9	80.6	324	639	402	161	339	800
Service occupations	50.8	71.2	218	4,487	306	4,351	253	8,838
Private household occupations	95.4	—	157	310	—	15	158	325
Launderers and ironers	—	—	—	0	—	0	—	0
Cooks, private household	—	—	—	5	—	0	—	5
Housekeepers and butlers	—	—	—	14	—	0	—	14
Child care workers, private households	98.7	—	129	150	—	2	127	152
Private household cleaners and servants	91.6	—	185	141	—	13	185	154
Protective service occupations	13.1	77.0	354	224	460	1,490	445	1,714
Supervisors, protective service occupations	8.9	—	—	16	643	163	622	179
Supervisors, firefighting and fire prevention	—	—	—	0	—	40	—	40
Supervisors, police and detectives	6.5	—	—	6	680	86	674	92
Supervisors, guards	—	—	—	10	—	37	—	47
Firefighting and fire prevention occupations	3.9	—	—	8	537	199	536	206
Fire inspection and fire prevention occupations	—	—	—	1	—	17	—	18
Firefighting occupations	3.7	—	—	7	537	182	537	188
Police and detectives	12.3	89.8	451	96	502	682	497	778
Police and detectives, public service	11.6	92.1	516	52	560	398	554	450
Sheriffs, bailiffs and other law enforce. officers	9.7	—	—	10	422	93	422	103
Correctional institution officers	15.0	—	—	34	439	191	431	226
Guards	18.9	86.4	248	104	287	446	280	551
Crossing guards	—	—	—	2	—	2	—	3
Guards and police, except public service	15.8	95.5	277	80	290	426	288	506
Protective service occupations, n.e.c.	—	—	—	23	—	18	—	41

MEDIAN WEEKLY EARNINGS OF WAGE AND SALARY WORKERS WHO USUALLY WORK FULL TIME, BY DETAILED OCCUPATION AND SEX, 1989 ANNUAL AVERAGES

(Numbers in thousands)

Occupation	Both sexes		Men		Women		Women's earnings as a percent of men's	Women as a Percent of total employed
	Number of workers	Median weekly earnings	Number of workers	Median weekly earnings	Number of workers	Median weekly earnings		
Service occupations, exc protective and pvt. household	6,799	234	2,846	262	3,953	219	83.6	58.1
Food preparation and service occupations	2,610	211	1,205	231	1,405	197	85.3	53.8
Supervisors, food preparation and service	238	268	98	306	141	236	77.1	59.2
Bartenders	175	239	90	266	84	220	82.7	48.0
Waiters and waitresses	597	203	142	246	455	190	77.2	76.2
Cooks, except short order	1,000	216	556	235	444	199	84.7	44.4
Short-order cooks	34	—	24	—	10	—	—	—
Food counter, fountain and related occupations	87	167	23	—	64	168	—	73.6
Kitchen workers, food preparation	53	191	15	—	38	—	—	71.7
Waiters'/waitresses' assistants	152	199	95	201	57	195	97.0	37.5
Miscellaneous food preparation occupations	273	195	162	199	111	189	95.0	40.7
Health service occupations	1,423	254	170	294	1,254	249	84.7	88.1
Dental assistants	121	280	0	—	121	280	—	100.0
Health aides, except nursing	282	277	51	308	231	269	87.3	81.9
Nursing aides, orderlies and attendants	1,020	244	118	289	902	239	82.7	88.4
Cleaning and bldg. service occupations, exc. household	1,967	261	1,279	285	687	224	78.6	34.9
Supervisors, cleaning and building service workers	143	346	90	400	53	268	67.0	37.1
Maids and housemen	385	213	88	240	297	205	85.4	77.1
Janitors and cleaners	1,406	269	1,068	281	337	239	85.1	24.0
Elevator operators	5	—	5	—	0	—	—	—
Pest control occupations	28	—	27	—	0	—	—	—

Occupation								
Personal service occupations	800	226	193	289	607	214	74.0	75.9
Supervisors, personal service occupations	19	—	8	—	11	—	—	—
Barbers	20	—	16	—	4	—	—	—
Hairdressers and cosmetologists	255	230	31	—	223	223	—	87.5
Attendants, amusement and recreation facilities	67	250	33	—	34	—	—	50.7
Guides	29	—	13	—	16	—	—	—
Ushers	4	—	3	—	1	—	—	—
Public transportation attendants	45	—	13	—	31	—	—	—
Baggage porters and bellhops	24	—	22	—	2	—	—	—
Welfare service aides	52	225	5	—	47	179	—	90.4
Child care workers, except private household	189	183	14	—	175	179	—	92.6
Personal service occupations, n.e.c.	95	233	34	—	61	219	—	64.2
Precision production, craft and repair occupations	11,326	454	10,413	469	913	311	66.3	8.1
Mechanics and repairers	3,936	457	3,798	457	138	470	102.8	3.5
Supervisors, mechanics and repairers	289	576	268	573	21	—	—	7.3
Mechanics and repairers, except supervisors	3,646	448	3,530	449	117	444	98.9	3.2
Vehicle and mobile equipment mechanics & repairers	1,436	415	1,426	415	10	—	—	0.7
Automobile mechanics	654	379	647	378	7	—	—	1.1
Bus, truck and stationary engine mechanics	281	430	281	430	0	—	—	0.0
Aircraft engine mechanics	120	532	119	533	1	—	—	0.8
Small engine repairers	46	—	45	—	1	—	—	—
Automobile body and related repairers	135	391	135	391	0	—	—	0.0
Aircraft mechanics, except engine	15	—	14	—	1	—	—	—
Heavy equipment mechanics	152	504	151	504	0	—	—	0.0
Farm equipment mechanics	33	—	33	—	0	—	—	—
Industrial machinery repairers	524	455	508	459	16	—	—	3.1
Machinery maintenance occupations	24	—	23	—	1	—	—	—
Electrical and electronic equipment repairers	619	538	569	541	50	512	94.6	8.1
Electronic repairers, communications and indust. equip.	132	471	124	475	8	—	—	6.1
Data processing equipment repairers	148	565	135	569	13	—	—	8.8

MEDIAN WEEKLY EARNINGS OF WAGE AND SALARY WORKERS WHO USUALLY WORK FULL TIME, BY DETAILED OCCUPATION AND SEX, 1989 ANNUAL AVERAGES

(Numbers in thousands)

Occupation	Both sexes		Men		Women		Women's earnings as a percent of men's	Women as a Percent of total employed
	Number of workers	Median weekly earnings	Number of workers	Median weekly earnings	Number of workers	Median weekly earnings		
Household appliance and power tool repairers	38	—	38	—	0	—	—	—
Telephone line installers and repairers	51	602	48	—	3	—	—	5.9
Telephone installers and repairers	195	583	174	590	21	—	—	10.8
Misc. electrical & electronic equipment repairers	56	489	50	493	5	—	—	8.9
Heating, air conditioning and refrig. mechanics	219	430	217	430	2	—	—	0.9
Miscellaneous mechanics and repairers	823	439	786	440	37	—	—	4.5
Camera, watch and musical instrument repairers	23	—	20	—	3	—	—	—
Locksmiths and safe repairers	14	—	14	—	0	—	—	—
Office machine repairers	58	416	55	422	3	—	—	5.2
Mechanical controls and valve repairers	14	—	13	—	1	—	—	—
Elevator installers and repairers	19	—	19	—	0	—	—	—
Millwrights	95	538	90	553	5	—	—	5.3
Specified mechanics and repairers, n.e.c.	407	424	390	424	17	—	—	4.2
Not specified mechanics and repairers	192	404	183	402	9	—	—	4.7
Construction trades	3,744	449	3,681	451	64	336	74.5	1.7
Supervisors, construction occupations	502	579	493	583	9	—	—	1.8
Suprvsrs, brickmasons, stonemasons and tile setters	7	—	7	—	0	—	—	—
Supervisors, carpenters and related workers	19	—	19	—	0	—	—	—
Supvsrs, electricians and power transmssn installers	35	—	35	—	0	—	—	—
Supervisors, painters, paperhangers and plasterers	8	—	8	—	0	—	—	—

Supervisors, plumbers, pipefitters and steamfitters	9	—	9	—	0	—	—	—
Supervisors, n.e.c.	423	569	414	575	8	—	—	1.9
Construction trades, except supervisors	3,242	424	3,188	425	55	321	75.5	1.7
Brickmasons and stonemasons	145	509	144	508	1	—	—	0.7
Tile setters, hard and soft	39	313	39	314	0	—	—	—
Carpet installers	57	396	56	396	1	—	—	1.8
Carpenters	914	403	903	405	11	—	—	1.2
Drywall installers	99	493	98	496	1	—	—	1.0
Electricians	618	556	604	556	14	—	—	2.3
Electrical power installers and repairers	105	353	105	357	0	—	—	0.0
Painters, construction and maintenance	294	—	285	—	10	—	—	3.4
Paperhangers	10	—	7	—	4	—	—	—
Plasterers	40	495	40	496	0	—	—	1.1
Plumbers, pipefitters and steamfitters	363	399	360	399	4	—	—	0.0
Concrete and terrazzo finishers	63	—	63	—	0	—	—	—
Glaziers	39	404	38	401	2	—	—	5.4
Insulation workers	56	—	54	—	3	—	—	—
Paving, surfacing and tamping equipment operators	13	353	13	356	0	—	—	1.0
Roofers	103	—	105	—	1	—	—	—
Sheet metal duct installers	34	625	33	626	2	—	—	0.0
Structural metalworkers	65	—	64	—	0	—	—	—
Drillers, earth	11	386	10	389	1	—	—	1.8
Construction trades, n.e.c.	169	555	166	561	3	—	—	2.2
Extractive occupations	134	—	131	—	3	—	—	—
Supervisors, extractive occupations	38	—	37	—	1	—	—	—
Drillers, oil well	27	—	26	—	1	—	—	—
Explosives workers	7	—	6	—	2	—	—	—
Mining machine operators	35	—	35	—	0	—	—	—
Mining occupations, n.e.c.	27	—	26	—	0	—	—	—

MEDIAN WEEKLY EARNINGS OF WAGE AND SALARY WORKERS WHO USUALLY WORK FULL TIME, BY DETAILED OCCUPATION AND SEX, 1989 ANNUAL AVERAGES

(Numbers in thousands)

Occupation	Both sexes		Men		Women		Women's earnings as a percent of men's	Women as a Percent of total employed
	Number of workers	Median weekly earnings	Number of workers	Median weekly earnings	Number of workers	Median weekly earnings		
Precision production occupations	3,512	450	2,804	492	708	295	60.0	20.2
Supervisors, production occupations	1,323	520	1,141	554	182	361	65.2	13.8
Precision metalworking occupations	829	481	784	487	45	—	—	5.4
Tool and die makers	141	593	138	595	3	—	—	2.1
Precision assemblers, metal	11	—	10	—	2	—	—	—
Machinists	446	465	430	469	16	—	—	3.6
Boilermakers	28	—	28	—	0	—	—	—
Precision grinders, fitters and tool sharpeners	14	—	13	—	0	—	—	—
Patternmakers and model makers, metal	3	—	3	—	0	—	—	—
Lay-out workers	6	—	5	—	1	—	—	—
Precious stones and metals workers (jewelers)	29	—	20	—	9	—	—	—
Engravers, metal	9	—	7	—	2	—	—	—
Sheet metal workers	139	464	130	478	9	—	—	6.5
Miscellaneous precision metalworkers	3	—	1	—	2	—	—	—
Precision woodworking occupations	53	331	44	—	10	—	—	18.9
Patternmakers and model makers, wood	3	—	3	—	0	—	—	—
Cabinet makers and bench carpenters	31	—	28	—	3	—	—	—
Furniture and wood finishers	19	—	13	—	6	—	—	—
Miscellaneous precision woodworkers	0	—	0	—	0	—	—	—
Precision textile, apparel and furnishings machine workers	123	274	68	310	55	239	77.1	44.7
Dressmakers	32	—	4	—	28	—	—	—
Tailors	41	—	26	—	15	—	—	—

Occupation								
Upholsterers	37	—	31	—	6	—	—	—
Shoe repairers	8	—	4	—	3	—	—	—
Apparel and fabric patternmakers	2	—	1	—	1	—	—	—
Miscellaneous precision apparel and fabric workers	3	—	1	—	2	—	—	—
Precision workers, assorted materials	485	325	216	402	269	294	73.1	55.5
Hand molders and shapers, except jewelers	21	—	19	—	2	—	—	—
Patternmakers, layout workers and cutters	25	308	19	—	6	—	—	62.1
Optical goods workers	58	—	22	—	36	—	—	—
Dental laboratory and medical appliance technicians	29	308	23	379	6	296	78.1	66.8
Bookbinders	41	—	18	—	23	—	—	—
Electrical and electronic equipment assemblers	286	—	95	—	191	—	—	—
Miscellaneous precision workers, n.e.c.	24	—	20	—	4	—	—	—
Precision food production occupations	328	299	225	351	103	222	63.2	31.4
Butchers and meat cutters	222	303	165	350	57	215	61.4	25.7
Bakers	78	276	48	—	31	—	—	39.7
Food batchmakers	27	—	12	—	15	—	—	—
Precision inspectors, testers and related workers	126	451	92	523	33	—	—	26.2
Inspectors, testers and graders	114	459	85	529	29	—	—	25.4
Adjusters and calibrators	12	—	8	—	4	—	—	—
Plant and system operators	245	523	234	523	11	—	—	4.5
Water and sewage treatment plant operators	57	438	52	432	4	—	—	7.0
Power plant operators	54	586	51	589	3	—	—	—
Stationary engineers	102	554	100	550	2	—	—	2.0
Miscellaneous plant and system operators	32	—	30	—	1	—	—	—
Operators, fabricators and laborers	15,166	323	11,349	366	3,817	252	68.9	25.2
Machine operators, assemblers and inspectors	7,530	313	4,526	379	3,004	251	66.2	39.9
Machine operators and tenders, except precision	4,937	301	2,934	364	2,003	238	65.4	40.6
Metalworking and plastic working machine operators	460	372	375	400	86	287	71.8	18.7
Lathe and turning machine set-up operators	22	—	22	—	0	—	—	—

MEDIAN WEEKLY EARNINGS OF WAGE AND SALARY WORKERS WHO USUALLY WORK FULL TIME, BY DETAILED OCCUPATION AND SEX, 1989 ANNUAL AVERAGES

(Numbers in thousands)

Occupation	Both sexes		Men		Women		Women's earnings as a percent of men's	Women as a Percent of total employed
	Number of workers	Median weekly earnings	Number of workers	Median weekly earnings	Number of workers	Median weekly earnings		
Lathe and turning machine operators	56	395	53	401	2	—	—	3.6
Milling and planing machine operators	12	—	11	—	1	—	—	—
Punching and stamping press machine operators	119	332	81	362	38	—	—	31.9
Rolling machine operators	14	—	12	—	2	—	—	—
Drilling and boring machine operators	28	—	17	—	11	—	—	—
Grinding, abrading, buffing and polishing machine opers.	143	374	117	396	26	—	—	18.2
Forging machine operators	19	—	18	—	1	—	—	—
Numerical control machine operators	5	—	5	—	0	—	—	—
Misc metal, plastic, stone and glass wkg mach ops.	44	—	39	—	4	—	—	—
Fabricating machine operators, n.e.c.	20	—	15	—	6	—	—	—
Metal and plastic processing machine operators	151	324	113	377	38	—	—	25.2
Molding and casting machine operators	93	306	65	359	28	—	—	30.1
Metal plating machine operators	30	—	24	—	6	—	—	—
Heat treating equipment operators	19	—	17	—	2	—	—	—
Misc. metal and plastic processing machine opers	8	—	6	—	2	—	—	—
Woodworking machine operators	147	286	124	296	23	—	—	15.6
Wood lathe, routing and planing machine operators	9	—	9	—	0	—	—	—
Sawing machine operators	82	273	70	290	12	—	—	14.6
Shaping and joining machine operators	9	—	7	—	2	—	—	—
Nailing and tacking machine operators	7	—	7	—	0	—	—	—
Miscellaneous woodworking machine operators	39	—	30	—	9	—	—	—

Printing machine operators	400	391	297	417	103	314	75.3	25.8
Printing machine operators	274	393	236	406	39	—	—	14.2
Photoengravers and lithographers	47	—	31	—	16	—	—	—
Typesetters and compositors	48	—	16	—	32	—	—	—
Miscellaneous printing machine operators	31	—	15	—	17	—	—	—
Textile, apparel and furnishings machine operators	1,179	218	251	281	928	208	74.0	78.7
Winding and twisting machine operators	72	281	21	—	50	257	—	69.4
Knitting, looping, taping and weaving mach. opers	46	—	19	—	28	—	—	—
Textile cutting machine operators	7	—	4	—	3	—	—	—
Textile sewing machine operators	698	205	64	245	633	202	82.4	90.7
Shoe machine operators	25	—	8	—	17	—	—	—
Pressing machine operators	98	213	28	—	69	195	—	70.4
Laundering and dry cleaning machine operators	157	211	61	228	97	205	89.9	61.8
Miscellaneous textile machine operators	76	281	45	—	31	—	—	40.8
Machine operators, assorted materials	2,580	322	1,760	368	820	265	72.0	31.8
Cementing and gluing machine operators	37	—	14	—	23	—	—	—
Packaging and filling machine operators	439	264	166	287	273	254	88.5	62.2
Extruding and forming machine operators	29	—	27	—	2	—	—	—
Mixing and blending machine operators	103	399	98	397	5	—	—	4.9
Separating, filtering and clarifying mach. opers	63	498	58	498	5	—	—	7.9
Compressing and compacting machine operators	24	—	17	—	7	—	—	—
Painting and paint spraying machine operators	169	322	149	330	20	—	—	11.8
Roasting and baking machine operators, food	4	—	3	—	0	—	—	—
Washing, cleaning and pickling machine operators	13	—	10	—	3	—	—	—
Folding machine operators	24	—	10	—	14	—	—	—
Furnace, kiln and oven operators, except food	94	436	91	439	3	—	—	3.2
Crushing and grinding machine operators	50	306	36	350	14	—	—	28.0
Slicing and cutting machine operators	209	311	155	350	54	232	66.3	25.8
Motion picture projectionists	1	—	1	—	0	—	—	—
Photographic process machine operators	67	311	33	—	34	—	—	50.7
Miscellaneous machine operators, n.e.c.	964	336	692	373	272	278	74.5	28.2
Machine operators, not specified	292	340	202	389	90	274	70.4	30.8

MEDIAN WEEKLY EARNINGS OF WAGE AND SALARY WORKERS WHO USUALLY WORK FULL TIME, BY DETAILED OCCUPATION AND SEX, 1989 ANNUAL AVERAGES

(Numbers in thousands)

Occupation	Both sexes		Men		Women		Women's earnings as a percent of men's	Women as a Percent of total employed
	Number of workers	Median weekly earnings	Number of workers	Median weekly earnings	Number of workers	Median weekly earnings		
Fabricators, assemblers and hand working occupations	1,756	343	1,201	390	555	266	68.2	31.6
Welders and cutters	561	403	523	405	38	—	—	6.8
Solderers and brazers	40	—	13	—	27	—	—	—
Assemblers	1,046	317	601	383	445	271	70.8	42.5
Hand cutting and trimming occupations	13	—	9	—	4	—	—	—
Hand molding, casting and forming occupations	15	—	15	—	1	—	—	—
Hand painting, coating and decorating occupations	28	—	16	—	11	—	—	—
Hand engraving and printing occupations	22	—	8	—	14	—	—	—
Hand grinding and polishing occupations	4	—	1	—	2	—	—	—
Miscellaneous hand working occupations	27	—	15	—	13	—	—	—
Production inspectors, testers, samplers and weighers	837	342	391	459	446	285	62.1	53.3
Production inspectors, checkers and examiners	682	358	314	479	369	293	61.2	54.1
Production testers	64	386	41	503	23	—	—	35.9
Production samplers and weighers	5	—	3	—	2	—	—	—
Graders and sorters, except agricultural	86	244	32	—	53	228	—	61.6
Transportation and material moving occupations	4,000	402	3,774	408	226	307	75.2	5.7
Motor vehicle operators	2,790	393	2,613	399	177	298	74.7	6.3
Supervisors, motor vehicle operators	76	466	67	503	10	—	—	1.8
Truck drivers, heavy	1,584	416	1,556	417	28	—	—	5.6
Truck drivers, light	586	319	553	324	33	—	—	5.6
Driver-sales workers	168	442	161	454	7	—	—	4.2

Occupation							
Bus drivers	211	368	127	395	85	326	82.5	40.3
Taxicab drivers and chauffeurs	124	306	114	320	10	—	—	8.1
Parking lot attendants	33	—	30	—	4	—	—	—
Motor transportation occupations, n.e.c.	7	—	7	—	0	—	—	—
Transportation occupations, except motor vehicle	163	629	158	634	5	—	—	3.1
Rail transportation occupations	123	659	119	663	4	—	—	3.3
Railroad conductors and yardmasters	38	—	37	—	1	—	—	—
Locomotive operating occupations	46	—	43	—	3	—	—	—
Railroad brake, signal and switch operators	30	—	30	—	0	—	—	—
Rail vehicle operators, n.e.c.	9	—	9	—	0	—	—	—
Water transportation occupations	39	—	39	—	1	—	—	—
Ship captains and mates, except fishing boats	22	—	22	—	0	—	—	—
Sailors and deckhands	12	—	12	—	0	—	—	—
Marine engineers	1	—	1	—	0	—	—	—
Bridge, lock and lighthouse tenders	4	—	4	—	1	—	—	—
Material moving equipment operators	1,047	403	1,004	406	44	—	—	4.2
Supervisors, material moving equipment operators	11	—	10	—	1	—	—	—
Operating engineers	201	484	199	483	3	—	—	1.5
Longshore equipment operators	1	—	1	—	0	—	—	—
Hoist and winch operators	15	—	13	—	1	—	—	—
Crane and tower operators	105	478	104	477	1	—	—	1.0
Excavating and loading machine operators	104	429	102	434	2	—	—	1.9
Grader, dozer and scraper operators	84	406	84	405	1	—	—	1.2
Industrial truck and tractor equipment operators	459	353	430	357	29	—	—	6.3
Miscellaneous material moving equipment operators	67	392	60	396	7	—	—	10.4
Handlers, equipment cleaners, helpers and laborers	3,636	288	3,049	297	587	241	81.1	16.1
Supervisors, handlers, equipment cleaners and laborers	12	—	12	—	0	—	—	—
Helpers, mechanics and repairers	27	—	27	—	1	—	—	—
Helpers, construction and extractive occupations	97	270	94	267	3	—	—	3.1
Helpers, construction trades	89	266	87	264	2	—	—	2.2

MEDIAN WEEKLY EARNINGS OF WAGE AND SALARY WORKERS WHO USUALLY WORK FULL TIME, BY DETAILED OCCUPATION AND SEX, 1989 ANNUAL AVERAGES

(Numbers in thousands)

Occupation	Both sexes		Men		Women		Women's earnings as a percent of men's	Women as a Percent of total employed
	Number of workers	Median weekly earnings	Number of workers	Median weekly earnings	Number of workers	Median weekly earnings		
Helpers, surveyor	6	—	6	—	0	—	—	—
Helpers, extractive occupations	2	—	2	328	0	—	—	2.5
Construction laborers	649	326	633	328	16	—	—	2.5
Production helpers	70	306	56	336	14	—	—	20.0
Freight, stock and material handlers	1,095	295	932	305	162	228	74.8	14.8
Garbage collectors	40	—	38	—	1	—	—	—
Stevedores	16	—	16	—	0	—	—	—
Stock handlers and baggers	387	232	298	249	89	202	81.1	23.0
Machine feeders and offbearers	84	304	63	312	21	—	—	25.0
Freight, stock and material handlers, n.e.c.	568	327	516	333	52	282	84.7	9.2
Garage and service station related occupations	167	225	159	227	8	—	—	4.8
Vehicle washers and equipment cleaners	215	232	189	233	25	—	—	11.6
Hand packers and packagers	263	252	107	289	156	224	77.5	59.3
Laborers, except construction	1,042	296	840	304	203	266	87.5	19.5
Farming, forestry and fishing occupations	1,383	246	1,222	252	162	211	83.7	11.7
Farm operators and managers	69	316	58	322	10	—	—	14.5
Farmers	8	—	6	—	1	—	—	—
Farm managers	61	320	52	337	9	—	—	14.8

Occupation							
Other agricultural and related occupations	1,231	238	1,083	244	148	207	84.8	12.0
Farm occupations, except managerial	615	219	533	223	83	196	87.9	13.5
Supervisors, farm workers	30	—	29	—	1	—	—	—
Farm workers	563	215	490	218	73	197	90.4	13.0
Marine life cultivation workers	3	—	3	—	0	—	—	—
Nursery workers	20	—	11	—	9	—	—	—
Related agricultural occupations	615	261	550	266	65	220	82.7	10.6
Supervisors, related agricultural occupations	62	379	59	382	3	—	—	4.8
Groundskeepers and gardeners, except farm	502	254	477	255	25	—	—	5.0
Animal caretakers, except farm	38	—	12	—	27	—	—	—
Graders and sorters, agricultural products	12	—	2	—	10	—	—	—
Inspectors, agricultural products	1	—	0	—	1	—	—	—
Forestry and logging occupations	65	307	63	306	2	—	—	3.1
Supervisors, forestry and logging occupations	3	—	2	—	0	—	—	—
Forestry workers, except logging	15	—	14	—	2	—	—	—
Timber cutting and logging occupations	47	—	47	—	0	—	—	—
Fishers, hunters, and trappers	19	—	18	—	1	—	—	—
Captains and other officers, fishing vessels	3	—	3	—	0	—	—	—
Fishers	16	—	15	—	1	—	—	—
Hunters and trappers	0	—	0	—	0	—	—	—

Note: Medians and percents are not shown where the base is under 50,000. Such cases are indicated by dashes.
Detail may not add to totals because of rounding.
N.e.c. = not elsewhere classified.
Source: U.S. Department of Labor, Bureau of Labor Statistics, Current Population Survey, 1989 annual averages.
Number of workers and median weekly earnings for occupations having 50,000 or more wage and salary workers were published in Employment and Earnings, January 1990. Other data are from BLS unpublished tabulations.

Index

Job Index

(Listings limited to jobs employing at least 500,000 people and not requiring a four-year college degree. See Appendix C for alphabetical listing of median weekly pay for 600 different jobs.)

A

Account and bill collectors, 63-65
Accoustical carpentry, 67
Acting, 83-85
Adjusters (customer complaints), 63-65
Advertising
 artists, 62-63
 clerks, 63-65
Agriculture, 6, 14, 54-57
Air-conditioning equipment, 82, 98-99
Aircraft repair and maintenance, 80, 98-99
Air Force, U.S., 97-100
Airline flight crews, 96, 99
Airline ground crews, 96, 99
Airline pilots, 96
Airline ticket agents, 63-65, 92, 96
Air traffic controllers, 92-93, 98
Amusement park attendants, 76-77, 92
Animal care, 54, 98
Apparel
 design, 59
 production, 86
 sales, 78
Appliances
 sales
 service, 4, 44-45, 67, 82, 85, 98
Armed Services, U.S., 97-100
Army, U.S., 97-100
Arts and crafts, 57-63, 85
Automobiles, 21, 80-81
Automotive maintenance,
 manufacturing and repairs, 21, 80-81, 98
Aviation, 63-65, 92-93, 96, 98, 99

B

Bakers, 86
Ballet, 83-85
Bank tellers, 63-65
Barbers, 21, 89
Bartending, 21, 29, 76
Beauticians, 90
Bicycle repairs, 83
Billing clerks, 63-65
Biological technicians, 95-96
Boat sales, 78
Bookkeepers, 63-65, 98
Book production, 86
Bricklaying, 66-67
Broadcast technicians, 93
Brokerage clerks, 63-65
Building custodians, 91
Building inspection, 67
Building maintenance, 5, 40, 44-46, 91
Bus drivers, 96-97
Business administration, 14, 63-65, 69, 77-79, 85, 98
Butchers, 86

C

Cabinet work, 88
Camera work, 61-62, 85, 98
Camp counselors, 92
Car delivery drivers, 97
Caretaking, 44-46, 56, 77
Car mechanics, 20, 80-81, 98
Carpentry, 44-46, 67, 85, 98
Carpet installation, 67
Cars, 21, 80-81
Car sales, 78